MOUNTAIN BIKE
CAMPING ADVENTURES

Bikepacking

ON THE
WILD TRAILS OF BRITAIN

LAURENCE McJANNET

WILD THINGS PUBLISHING

MOUNTAIN BIKE
CAMPING ADVENTURES

Bikepacking

ON THE
WILD TRAILS OF BRITAIN

CONTENTS

THE SELECTION

THE REGIONS

ABERDEEN

26

24

25

DUNDEE

EDINBURGH

NEWCASTLE

22

23

21

20

HULL

MANCHESTER

19

16

15

28

29

BIRMINGHAM

18

17

09

27

30

CARDIFF

BRISTOL

10

08

LONDON

11

02

14

DOVER

06

03

01

PORTSMOUTH

SOUTHAMPTON

05

04

12

07

13

PLYMOUTH

RIDE DATA

NO	CHAPTER NAME	COUNTY / AREA	TRAIN STATIONS (DISTANCE)
1	The Deverills in the Detail	Wiltshire	Tisbury / Warminster
2	Avon Calling	Bath, North East Somerset	Frome / Avoncliff
3	Cresting the Quantocks	Quantocks, Somerset	Williton [1]
4	A Studland Sortie	Purbecks, Dorset	Corfe Castle / Norden [2]
5	Jurassic Roller Coaster	East Devon	Honiton (5km)
6	Valley of the Rocks - an Exmoor Epic	Exmoor	Barnstaple (17km)
7	A Taste of the Tors	Dartmoor	Exeter St Davids (13km) / Newton Abbot (16km)
8	A Green Ribbon through the Big Smoke	South London	Kew Gardens / Hampton
9	London's Greenest Gateway	Epping Forest, Essex	Forest Gate / Cheshunt
10	Finding Efrafa	Hampshire	Bedwyn / Overton
11	Wonder Weald	Kent	Wye
12	The Beautiful South	Sussex	Chichester / Arundel
13	Sanctuary on the Solent	Isle of Wight	Lymington Pier
14	Stane Street Revisited	Surrey	Ockley / Epsom
15	From Fens to Forest	Norfolk	Harling Road (2km) / Thetford (8km)
16	A Drift through Wild Midland Meadows	Rutland	Bottesford / Oakham
17	A Wold Away	Cotswolds	Cheltenham Spa (10km)
18	Malvern's Great Sentinel	Malverns	Great Malvern
19	Riding on the Edge	Peak District	Bamford (3km) / Edale
20	Yorkshire's Bleak Beauty	North York Moors	Pickering (21km)
21	High Hills, Deep Dales	Yorkshire Dales	Redmire [3] (8km) / Kirkby Stephen (26km)
22	Rising to the Challenge	Buttermere, Lake District	Whitehaven (20km)
23	Taming the Wilds of Windermere	Windermere, Lake District	Windermere (8km) / Kendal (21km)
24	A Room with a View	Isle of Mull	Oban
25	Between a Loch and a Hard Place	Loch Lomond	Arrochar & Tarbet / Crianlarich
26	Mountain Bikes and Bothy Nights	Cairngorms	Pitlochry / Blair Atholl
27	Surf's Up	Gower	Swansea
28	Touching the Sky	Snowdonia	Pont Croesor / Beddgelert [4]
29	Break for the Border	Trans-Wales North	Rhyl (2km) / Broome (11km)
30	Along the Edge of the Realm	Trans-Wales South	Broome (11km) / Chepstow (2km)

Notes: (1) West Somerset Railway   (2) Swanage Railway   (3) Wensleydale Railway   (4) Welsh Highland Railway

START / FINISH POINT	DISTANCE, KM	HEIGHT GAIN, M	OFF-ROAD %	DIFFICULTY
Tisbury / Horningsham	35.3	786	80	**
Frome / Avoncliff	44.5	955	65	**
Holford	44.1	1260	80	***
Studland	43.9	954	80	***
Gittisham	34.2	858	70	***
Simonsbath	75.0	2117	85	****
nr. Postbridge	55.8	1691	75	*****
Kew-Hampton	31.5	329	85	*
Forest Gate / Cheshunt	30.8	379	90	*
Great Bedwyn / Overton	38.6	659	85	**
Wye	52.2	917	75	**
Chichester / Arundel	45.0	937	85	***
Yarmouth	42.6	884	75	***
Ockley / Epsom	39.1	929	80	***
Holme-next-the-Sea / Knettishall Heath	73.5	750	70	**
Bottesford / Oakham	50.2	428	80	**
Birdlip	24.0	554	75	**
Great Malvern	45.2	1624	85	***
Heatherdene / Edale	31.8	871	70	****
Helmsley	51.5	1148	70	****
Fremington	37.1	1317	80	****
Buttermere	28.0	918	90	****
Hawkshead	22.2	696	85	**
Tobermory / Tomsleibhe	40.2	669	80	***
Arrochar & Tarbet / Crianlarich	34.6	1043	90	****
Pitlochry / Blair Atholl	51.1	1279	85	****
Swansea	67.7	1358	70	***
Prenteg / Snowdon summit	32.8	1758	75	****
Prestatyn / Clun	192.6	4444	65	*****
Clun / Sedbury	179.2	4236	55	*****

"NOT ALL THOSE
WHO WANDER
ARE LOST"

JRR TOLKEIN, THE LORD OF THE RINGS

BIKEPACKING

Welcome to the wonderful world of bikepacking, the natural fusion of mountain biking and lightweight camping, inspired by the original spirit of the first off-road adventure riders in 1970s California. The chances are, if you have picked up this book, you already enjoy riding off-road, wild camping, cycle-camping or backpacking by foot, then you will find 'bikepacking' exhilarating, liberating and a great way to explore Britain.

Bikepacking adventures are self-supported, two-wheeled, overnight forays, off the tarmac roads and into the countryside or wilderness on tracks and ancient byways. In this book you will find a collection of my favourite off-road bikepacking routes from across Britain – from the epic and remote to the surprisingly accessible and child-friendly. And you don't need lots of fancy kit; a growing number of mountain bikers, hikers and wild campers are discovering that, with as little as an old mountain or hybrid bike, a bed mat, sleeping bag and a bivvy bag, a whole new world begins to open up: a vast, often wild but always beautiful landscape just waiting to be discovered. And the best way to do so is on two wheels, wild camping on the way. In doing so, you can journey greater distances and explore more remote trails than you ever could on a day ride.

The 'ride' itself becomes more than just that too – it becomes a journey of discovery, not only of the natural world around us, but of ourselves as well. We learn a lot when we step outside our comfort zone, eschewing a warm bed and our mod cons for a night or two, and riding further than we have before into the British wilderness, expanding our horizons literally and metaphorically.

Just as the history of cycle touring can be traced back to the advent of the first road bicycle, so too have there been bikepackers as long as there have been mountain bikes. They just didn't know it. The beautiful thing about cycling, in whatever form it takes, is that it imbues the rider with an urge to pedal off into the unknown.

It wasn't long before mountain biking's pioneers on the US West Coast, guys like Joe Breeze, Gary Fisher and Otis Guy – who in the 1970s had adapted old one-speed coaster-braked 'Clunker' bikes with wide tyres for racing downhill tracks – felt the urge to strike out from their familiar trails along Mount Tamalpais, into the wilds of Marin County, California, and beyond. Though still using parts from 1950s Schwinn Excelsiors, Breeze began building dedicated lightweight mountain bike frames – called Breezers, naturally. The rest, as they say, is history.

It was a natural progression for these first mountain bikers to take their Breezers and Clunkers east into the mountains, blazing a trail for the next generation of riders to follow, and carving out epic routes through the vast American wilderness. Bikepackers on this side of the Atlantic can only dream about the likes of the VMBT (Virginia Mountain Bike Trail) a 770km route across the Allegheny and Blue Ridge Mountains, or the 1280km desert odyssey from Utah to Mexico that is the Arizona Trail. Yet the British Isles has all this and more in microcosm – a wonderful distillation of ridge, lake, mountain, valley and coast, all of which a weekend ride and camp can encompass. It's an island that is almost tailor-made for off-road adventure rides.

FAT TYRES & CAMPFIRES

The joy of bikepacking, I've always found, is not only the feeling of going 'off-grid' and being self-reliant but how, by taking the paths less travelled, the ones that seemingly lead nowhere or have no immediate destination, your tyres can be the first to touch that trail in weeks, months – years even. Spending a night in the woods close to home can lend a whole new perspective to a loop that you ride often, while continuing along a trail you've always meant to explore further, camping en route, can lead you into wonderful uncharted territory just a day's ride from your front door. At the other end of the spectrum, with a little planning, you can cover huge distances on multi-day rides, finding your own food and water as you go, and lending such journeys the feel of odysseys. In our increasingly stressful and sedentary lives, a night spent sleeping under the stars amid a ride into unfamiliar terrain serves as a wonderful reboot for our system and the way we regard things that are important to us – family, friends, the world around us.

There's nothing more relaxing than falling asleep to the hoot of a distant owl or the chirrup of crickets, or more invigorating than waking up to the view of rolling hills, rocky peaks, placid lakes or waves breaking on some sandy shore. If the smell of last night's wood smoke still lingers in your hair, and you have a companion to share the experience with, so much the better. All you need to do is stuff your few belongings into packs on your bikes, remount and continue the adventure.

WILD CAMPING

While road cycle tourers tend to stop at pubs, B&Bs and roadside accommodation on their journeys (though of course many do camp at campsites), bikepackers are often more remote, immersed in the wilderness so a wild camp is the natural, sometimes only, option. But, outside of Dartmoor and Scotland, where wild camping is permitted, the chances are you'll be camping on someone's land. While there are many discussions to be had about where you can legitimately wild camp (those fishing on the foreshore – the area of shoreline exposed between high and low tides – or navigating rivers and canals at night have historically been granted the right to sleep there), the bottom line is that wild camping may be trespass, but trespass is a civil offence, not a criminal offence, nor a police matter. However, 'reasonable force' can be used to remove you by the most convenient route if you refuse to leave having been asked.

You do have some rights if you are there by necessity, for instance if you have fallen sick or twisted an ankle, but always try to ask the landowner's permission first, and if there are signs asking you not to camp, obey them. You should always be prepared to move on if asked by the landowner or their agent and if you seek to actively disrupt people on that land who are going about their business (e.g. camping in the middle of a football pitch) or are offensive, then you could be charged with 'aggravated trespass', which is a criminal offence.

With a little discretion and common sense it's easy to find appropriate places to camp, and appropriate ways to do it. A simple bivvy bag behind a hedge will almost always go unnoticed – a tent in a crop field may be asking for trouble. Tarp shelters or bashas are useful in bad weather, and can be pulled down in minutes. And although a tent is the most obtrusive option, the microlight varieties that work best for bikepacking tend to be small, low, simple structures. It's not like you're erecting a yurt in someone's field.

Though it's always best to be out of sight of houses, you'll be surprised how many great wild camping spots can be found close to towns and villages. If you cycle away from the houses, find a bridleway or footpath to push along, then depart from that to find hedgerows, trees or even open downland, and make sure you are not in view. You can be treated to some wonderful views while remaining entirely anonymous. If you are away from any path you are unlikely to be disturbed or cause a disturbance yourself. If you are new to sleeping wild this is often the best way to start out. You are not in so wild a spot as to be completely isolated, and the knowledge that civilisation is a few fields away can be comforting at first. I can guarantee that soon you'll want to expand your horizons and will be planning a far-flung wilderness escape before long. And if you are challenged in the evening, just say sorry, offer to leave, but ask if £10 would be enough to allow you to stay the night. Better still – ask before you camp. As long as you are out of sight of roads or dwellings, you arrive late and leave early, cause no damage and leave no trace, and stay no more than a night, then you won't bother anyone.

There are a number of other exceptions and ideas which is worth knowing about too. The 2003 Land Reform Act restored the right to wild camp throughout Scotland, so you can plan wild rides north of the border unfettered by laws and regulations. Dartmoor too has a very progressive attitude to wild camping (though camp well away from any site of antiquity). Many other mountain areas are tolerant of wild camping, especially if you are above 450m and more than an hour's walk from the nearest road. The right to 24-hour fishing, bait digging and navigation in England was enshrined under the Magna Carta in 1215. As such you can sleep on a canal barge, while on a canoe or kayak trip, or while fishing on the foreshore. If you're carrying a trowel (which can be useful for digging toilets and burying ashes) you can even justify your presence near water as a bait digger. Buying a bar meal from a pub or produce from a farm shop is often seen as a fair exchange for a night's camping, and you could ask if they have a field, though more often than not it's far from wild. Or for a nominal membership fee the Backpackers Club in Britain provides a list of pubs and farms where you can camp free of charge. It's worth joining the Mountain Bothies Association too. Though you'll never be asked to prove membership at one of the many maintained but unmanned bothies in remote parts of Scotland and the north of England, your £20 will support the wonderful work the volunteers do to keep them open and habitable throughout the year. Check out the Scottish rides in Mull (ride no.24), Loch Lomond (25) and the Cairngorms (26), all of which visit a wonderful MBA bothy (mountainbothies.org.uk).

RIDE, EAT, SLEEP, REPEAT

As with any new niche in cycling — be it cross-country, trials, all-mountain, downhill or enduro — the industry has certainly been quick to embrace bikepacking.

With a view to creating modern bikes that are capable of hauling kit and carrying a rider in relative comfort over long distances and varying terrain, the industry now boasts specific 'backcountry', 'gravel', 'drop-bar adventure' and 'fat' bikes. Each is a variation of a traditional mountain bike or cyclo-cross bike, and tends to be rigid (i.e. no suspension either front or back) to make the bike more efficient on longer journeys while the 'fat' bike features balloon-like tyres and reinforced rims for increased stability and traction (they were originally developed for riding in snowy or sandy conditions). The fat tyres also provide some suspension in their own right. The availability and innovation of fat bikes, soft bags and other gear is beginning to popularise a sport that is still in its infancy and to lend it recognition.

But don't think that you'll need to spend big to get into bikepacking. If you already own a bike that can be ridden off-road, then you are ready to head for the hills. If you go camping, however infrequently, the chances are you already own much of the equipment you'll need, and you really don't need very much. An alternative is to hire the full kit, including a modern fat bike, and have it delivered to the start of your adventure, a service offered by Adventure Pedlars.

Through experience you'll figure out what would be worth investing in, in terms of bike components, clothing and camping kit. After your initial forays close to home you may want to strike out further afield, ride faster, further and for longer, take on more challenging routes or camp later in the year.

Here are a few ideas for kit that will make your life easier and may make your ride and night's sleep more enjoyable.

THE BIKE: The best bike for bikepacking is the one you already own. You don't need a frame with eyelets or rack mounts for panniers, and even a road bike can be fitted with wider, more robust tyres to cope with canal towpaths and paved bridleways. A hybrid (a compromise between road and mountain bike) can cope with most rides too, though a proper off-road hardtail (knobbly tyres and front but no rear suspension) will give you more scope for planning longer, more technical rides. I find there's no better bike than a rigid hardtail, the original mass-produced mountain bike, and the kind that has been left neglected in many people's garages for a decade or more. With no suspension forks to compress, you don't have to worry about your tyre catching a bag slung under your handlebars. For the same reason a full suspension rig is probably too much bike for most bikepacking adventures, unless you have dedicated frame bags. Too many moving parts can be problematic when you have luggage slung under the front, centre and back of the frame. Big-wheeled bikes (with 29in or the new 'standard' 650b wheels) are great for manoeuvrability but can have limited clearance for hanging luggage slings under bars and seat-posts.

CARRYING THINGS: You'll need a backpack of some kind, around 30 litres is perfect, and ideally with double straps rather than a messenger bag with a single strap. Try to keep as much load off your back as possible, though a backpack is ideal for carrying tools, hydration, cameras and other items you might want regular access to. You'll need at least one bag attached to the frame to carry your overnight kit, though two or three spread evenly across the bike work better. Knowing the British weather it's best that these are waterproof (drybags are available from most outdoor retailers and come in a variety of

BACK PACK:
Rain jacket, spare base layer, spare trousers/leggings
Puncture repair kit, tyre levers, mini pump
Camping knife/fork/spoon
Spare chain and power link
Water bottle and Camelbak (in bag)
Extra self-adhesive tyre patches
Selection of multi-tool kits
Hand-held or head torch
Spare brake pads
Bar-mounted light
Compass

BAR MOUNTED POUCH
Energy gels and mid-ride snacks
Compact camera

SADDLE BAG:
Three-season sleeping bag
Spare foldable tyre

TOP TUBE BAG:
2x rope and carabiner clips
Parachute silk hammock

BAR-MOUNTED DRYBAG:
All-in-one stove, pan and gas canister
Dried food and powdered drinks
Sleeping bag liner
Inflatable sleeping mat
Tarp with cord and pegs
Spare inner tube
Thermos cup
Hip flask
Bivvy bag
Coffee filter

sizes, with loops, eyelets or straps to give you loads of mounting options). However, if it's the middle of a dry dusty summer a bin bag might get you through (it worked for me on my first adventure ride). Bungee cords, Velcro or adjustable straps will keep them in place, but I've seen cord, string and even plumbing clips do the job just as well.

SLEEPING: A simple bedroll or mat and sleeping bag will do. Don't worry if it's not a down or three-seasons bag; whatever you have will do for now. Sleeping mats are light but can be cumbersome to carry – though you can strap them under your bars or saddle if you have room. Spare clothes in a dry bag or bin bag make a luxurious pillow.

EATING/DRINKING: Take food that doesn't need cooking at first, or eat before you go. If your first adventure rides are near your home you can have breakfast when you get back. Two 750ml water bottles should be ok for short rides.

FIXING THINGS: Whether it's for you or the bike, there are certain remedies you shouldn't be without. A torch is always useful, a simple tool kit, pump, tyre levers and spare inner tubes will keep you on the move. A basic first aid kit and phone will let your loved ones sleep a little easier – remember to tell them where you are going and when you'll be back.

CLOTHING: Unless the forecast guarantees dry weather, take a waterproof jacket. It needn't be a cycling-specific cut; you just need something to keep you dry until you can find shelter to make camp. Remember to bring a number of extra layers. Sleep in what you wear during the ride, and add layers as you need to. Woolly hats are invaluable, as is a spare pair of socks. Merino wool base layers, and a down jacket or gilet, pack down small but provide bags of insulation. A cycle-specific waterproof jacket will keep you drier and more comfortable for longer on the bike.

Waterproof shorts or trousers could be wise too, as well as padded cycle shorts. A camping stove and pan with gas canister (or all-in-one), ceramic mug, fork and spoon – hot food and drink add a whole new dimension to wild camping, and are the simplest way to make it more enjoyable. My favourites are Alpkit's BruKit all-in-one and the MSR Pocket Rocket stove. A tarpaulin shelter (generic ones are fine but most camping-specific ones have reinforced eyelets for pegging out – again Alpkit make particularly good ones) and pegs will give you loads of options to help stay dry. A proper breathable bivvy bag wicks away moisture and keeps you more comfortable than a survival bag. A Camelbak or similar water bladder for drinking on the move. Oh yes, and a hip flask…

BIKE ACCESSORIES: A handlebar harness for mounting a drybag under your bars. You can usually fit a 12 or 16 litre bag under there, with plenty of space for a stove, food, bivvy and tarp. A mid-frame bag to hang under the top tube (if you have a full suspension frame you may need a tailor-made one to make room for the shock). A saddle sling or bag to fit another dry bag. There should be space to get your sleeping bag and even a spare foldable tyre in here. Alpkit, Apidura and Wildcat Gear all make great, dedicated waterproof frame bags. Adjustable bottle cage mounts – with a frame bag in place there won't be much room for the bottle cage in its usual place. These let you mount your water bottle underneath your downtube, on your fork legs, bars or seat-post – SKS make a great one that will fit around all but the fattest frame tubes. A top-tube or stem-mounted 'fuel cell' or 'gas tank' – perfect for mid-ride stacks or compact cameras. A wider ratio cassette for more flexible gearing under load – the Wolfstooth 42T cog is a great example. A spare foldable tyre, as a burst sidewall can put an immediate end to your ride (though a small cut-up section of milk carton between inner tube and tyre side wall can get you home in an emergency). Ergonomic bars, grips and saddle will keep you comfy on the trail for longer. Look for bars with a greater sweep than usual (such as the Jones Bend H-Bar or On-One's Fleegle bar). Try 'stubbie' bar ends of the likes of Ergon's grips for multiple hand positions.

TENTS AND TARPS: A microlight one- or two-man tent or specific shelter. Ditch the tarp and bivvy and you'll be able to carry on bikepacking right through the year (well, almost!) Most are small enough to be slung under your handlebars. I've used the Vango Tempest, but the MLD Trailstar and Golite Shangri-La are well worth a look. Or for unforgettable forest camping you could try Tentsile's range of suspended tree tents. A head-torch is much more practical than a handheld one. Even during a prolonged dry spell I would take an orange survival bag, (available from many specialist outdoor shops), to protect my sleeping bag from rips and tears as much as bad weather. It's another layer, no matter how uninsulated, with which to trap warm air, and it will keep moisture and rain at bay too.

OTHER BITS: Mobile phone, spare battery and spot tracker, dehydrated foodstuffs (any food you add hot water too tends to be compact and light but very satisfying), mid-ride snacks (fig rolls, flapjacks, jelly babies, energy bars or gels all work well), tea, coffee (a moka pot or individual filters) or hot chocolate sachets, and porridge sachets, the breakfast of champions.

Investing in new kit as and when you can will inevitably lighten the load you have to carry and consequently make your bike easier to handle and therefore more enjoyable to ride. Another option is to make sure key pieces of equipment serve more than one purpose. A heavyweight sleeping bag can just be used for sleeping, while a lighter bag and down jacket have the same result, with the jacket useful during the day too.

TARPOLOGY

Next to tents, the tarp is the most important bit of shelter the wilderness traveller carries. For a solo/tandem little tarp, go for nothing less than 3m long and 2m wide. Use a big tarp for groups, the bigger the better, up to about 5m max and the same wide. PU proofed nylon is pretty much as good as it gets: strong, light, compact, versatile, dries fast and you can patch it with gaffer tape. Silicon proofing is good but heavy driving rain will spit through. Avoid canvas, it's immensely heavy, when it gets wet stays wet and if you touch it, it will dribble through. Go for webbing loops and plenty of them (look for sound bar-tacking and gate-stitch), brass or alloy grommets will rip out, especially with builders tarps

WHERE TO PITCH

In the Scottish highlands or Scandinavia flat ground is at a premium and finding any may well dictate the location. But here are some points to consider and places to avoid, a.k.a. the 5 "Ws":

WIND. A breeze of 3 mph will keep the midges grounded – excellent! A gale will turn your tarp into a hang glider – not so good.

WATER. If you can be choosy, avoid frost-hollows, cold air current gullies, moss, bogs and smooth bare earth that was once mud and will be again!

WILDLIFE. In the wilds avoid rigging it over a game trail! Enough said.

WIGGLIES. Check for insects and snakes and remember, having swept aside an ant trail it takes precisely the time to re-establish as it does for you to completely unpack and lay out your sleeping bag.

WIDOWMAKERS. Look up and check for dead branches, avoid beech trees (summer branch break is a very real hazard), crumbling walls, cliff faces etc. These things may do more than just flatten your kettle!

KNOTS AND LASHINGS

If you haven't got mini-krabs, ratchet straps, guy tensioners etc and can't tie knots, learn! You only need:

A larks head: to put lines on loops

A wagoner's hitch to create a taut line

A round turn and 2 half hitches to tie off on a tree or log

A taut-line hitch to fix the tarp edge to the taut line or to tension guys

And make all knots slippery, i.e. with the end pulled through in a loop to make undoing them simple and to save dragging the whole lot through when tying a short belay with a long line. Learn the Siberian (Evenk) hitch, it immediately identifies you as a 'Tarp Meister' and dissuades helpful comments as to how they would have rigged it differently, better etc. You can tie it even when wearing gloves.

by Jed Yarnold
True North Outdoor, Witney, Oxfordshire
www.truenorthoutdoor.co.uk
01993 822 954 - 07904 144 546

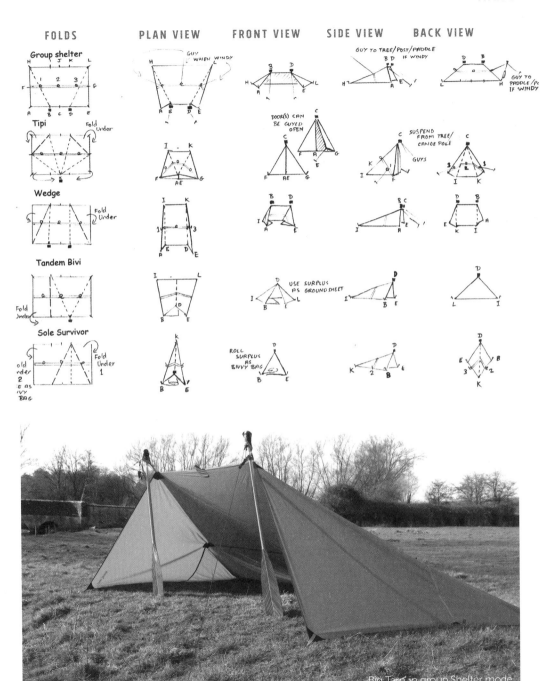

FOLDS	PLAN VIEW	FRONT VIEW	SIDE VIEW	BACK VIEW

Group shelter

Tipi

Wedge

Tandem Bivi

Sole Survivor

Big Tarp in group Shelter mode

PLANNING A RIDE

There is a vast network of paths, tracks, drovers' ways, Roman roads and forest trails criss-crossing our countryside, from the humble bridleway to long-distance waymarked routes. Britain has one of the highest densities of bridleways and byways in the world, so it's easier to plan an off-road ride than you might think. In Scotland you can cycle anywhere and many National Parks in England and Wales will provide information on specific routes – Dartmoor, the Peak District and Yorkshire Dales are particularly strong, as well as Snowdonia and the Brecon Beacons. There are several National Trails you can cycle, such as the Ridgeway, South Downs Way and the Peddars Way (www.nationaltrail.co.uk), as well as numerous other long-distance paths. Though these are usually waymarked, there are some, including the Peak District's Pennine Bridleway, the Great Glen Way from Fort William to Inverness and the Two Moors Way which runs through Exmoor and Dartmoor that feel particularly wild!

There is also a wealth of trails to be found throughout our many forests. While the New Forest in Dorset, Nottinghamshire's Sherwood Pines and Thetford Forest in East Anglia are great for riders of all abilities, the more experienced could look to Whinlatter in Cumbria, Kielder in Northumberland or Gloucestershire's Forest of Dean for some memorable bikepacking adventures. For more information on mountain biking in English forests go to www.forestry.gov.uk; for Wales it is now www.naturalresources.wales. Just remember to check local bylaws when planning to wild camp in forests – you won't be allowed to light fires on Forestry Commission land, for example.

You'll also be surprised how many bridle paths snake around the outskirts of many villages, towns or even cities before joining the lattice-like network of rights of way that cover our countrywide (commons, canal towpaths and riverside paths are all good opportunities for beginning more urban explorations – see the Bath and London rides for instance.

When planning, choose between a loop to take you back to your point of origin – the train station, perhaps, or your camper or car – or a point-to-point ride, which can give the ride more of a feeling of a journey, but you will need two cars if not starting and finishing at a station.

I recently learned that cartography is no longer taught in England's colleges and universities so it seems this country's map makers are something of a dying breed. I for one won't be relinquishing my hard copy OS maps any time soon – both 1:25,000 Explorers (the orange ones) and 1:50,000 Landrangers (the purple ones) are invaluable for giving you the bigger picture of routes, landscape and topography – and you can now buy the digital versions to carry on your phone or tablet, from Viewranger, MemoryMap or RouteBuddy. There are lots of useful digital tools for creating routes and for navigation. Bing Maps and Streetmap are almost unique in providing OS mapping for free (though it won't work on a mobile device) and it's well worth checking the satellite images and photos available with Google Maps.

Do always stick to rights of way for bikes – bridleways, towpaths, BOATs, RUPPs, ORPAs (see box), as well as lanes, unsurfaced tracks and minor roads. Apart from the short dashed pink lines on Landranger maps (they are green on Explorers) that denote footpaths (which you should avoid or dismount on) the world is your oyster.

Use the routes in this book as ideas, as a basis for creating your own routes and for extending them to create longer trails with other waymarked routes. Sometimes it can be really rewarding not to plan at all. Just take a train an hour or so's ride from home, and use your map and compass to get back, examining trail types and landscape contours to seek out the best potential trails, scenery and views. You may have to ride on roads from time to time to head in the general direction of home, but sometimes you'll stumble upon amazing trails that will keep you on your way – a perfect recipe for a unique adventure ride. Serendipitous twists (and occasional follies) can only make these rides all the more memorable!

Why not enter an off-road race, ride to it the night before and wild camp just off the race trail? By the time the other competitors arrive you'll be rested, raring to go, and may even have had a chance to get a practice lap or two in. At the very least you'll have something to talk about on the starting grid. As the UK bikepacking scene starts to gain momentum, dedicated events are starting to pop up across the country. Check out Alpkit's Big Shakeout weekend, Adventure Pedlars' events and the Welsh Ride Thing, among others.

The routes in this book have suggested inns, campsites Ⓐ and bivvy spots Ⓒ. Please do not bivvy without attempting to seek the landowner's permission

OS EXPLORER SYMBOLS (ORANGE, 1:25,000)		OS LANDRANGER SYMBOLS (PURPLE, 1:50,000)
- - - - - - - - - -	**FOOTPATH:** no cycling	· - - - - - - - - -
— — — — —	**BRIDLEWAY:** horses and cycle	— — — — —
+++++++	**RESTRICTED BYWAY:** closed to motorised vehicles	-+-+-+-+-+
-+-+-+-	**BYWAY OPEN TO ALL TRAFFIC:** (BOAT) including motorised vehicles	· - · - · - · -
· · · ·	**OTHER ROUTE WITH PUBLIC ACCESS:** (ORPA) usually cycleable	· · · ·
- - - - -	**UNDESIGNATED TRACK:** maybe private	— — — — —
· · · ·	**CYCLE ROUTE:** traffic-free	• • • • •
☐1	**CYCLE ROUTE:** Sustrans National Cycle Network	○ ○ ○ ○ ○

It's one thing planning where to go, it's quite another deciding when. Trail conditions can vary dramatically depending on the weather and season, so it pays to research local terrain and rock type. Mountain bike forums such as singletrackworld.com offer great ways to get in touch with local riders to find out more about the places you are planning to ride. Typically forest trails and open moors will become more difficult in wetter conditions, chalk and limestone may be a little slipperier but tend to drain standing water away better.

Depending on the season you may want to leave your food at home and forage for a meal, if you know where and when to look – adventure rides don't get more self-supported than this. Different seasons bring other benefits and drawbacks too. From March you'll have extra daylight for longer rides, April's a good time to look for wild mushrooms (but only if you know what you're doing), May is wild garlic time, June's summer solstice (or any full moon) is the perfect time for night rides. July is great for hazelnuts, August for wild strawberries, and September for blackberries – as well as the warmest sea swims you'll have all year. October is deer rutting season (best avoid riding near herds), and in Scotland it pays to check before riding through estate-managed land.

Perhaps the most important thing to consider is your environmental impact. Stick to singletrack and try to avoid riding on saturated trails, which will minimise damage, though the latter is easier said than done. Use only dead wood for a fire if you need one, and make sure you bury human waste well away from trails and water sources. As bikepacking grows it pays to consider the sustainability of the sport and foster an environmental stewardship that will grow as the sport does. Leaving the wild places as you found them or better still clearing up after those who may have been before you is a small price to pay for whichever wonderful 'room' with a view you choose for the night.

BOOKS AND RESOURCES

ROUTE BOOKS

Great Britain Mountain Biking, Tom Fenton & Andy McCandlish, Vertebrate Publishing, 2014

The Good Mountain Biking Guide – England & Wales, Active Maps, Pioneer Partners, 2011

Traffic-Free Cycle Trails, Nick Cotton, Vertebrate Publishing, 2014

Lost Lanes, Jack Thurston, Wild Things Publishing, 2013

Lost Lanes Wales, Jack Thurston, Wild Things Publishing, 2015

Britain By Bike, Jane Eastoe, Batsford, 2010

The Ultimate UK Cycle Route Planner, Excellent Books, 2016

Sustrans' Traffic-Free Cycle Rides, Sustrans, 2015

Vinter's Railway Gazetteer - A Guide to Britain's Old Railways that You Can Walk or Cycle, Jeff Vinter, History Press, 2011

Cycle Tours, Nick Cotton, Cordee - local route guides with Ordnance Survey mapping

Rough Ride Guides series (roughrideguides.co.uk)

Cicerone's portfolio of regional mountain bike guide books

WILD CAMPING BOOKS

The Book of the Bivvy, Ronald Turnbull, Cicerone (second edition, 2015)

The Bivouac Handbook, Rob Reaser, RBC, 2012 (eBook)

Lightweight Camping, John Traynor, Cicerone, 2010

Microadventures, Alastair Humphreys, HarperCollins, 2014

Extreme Sleeps - Adventures of a Wild Camper, Phoebe Smith, Summersdale, 2013

The Natural Explorer, Tristan Gooley, Hachette 2013

Wild Camping, Stephen Neale, Bloomsbury, 2015

The Wild Places, Robert Macfarlane, Granta Books, 2008

ONLINE RESOURCES

bikepacking.com - great for bikepacking culture, international inspiration and imagery, but only a few routes in the UK

bearbonesbikepacking.co.uk - UK-specific website including a popular forum, kit reviews, shop and information on bikepacking events

bikepackersmagazine.com - another US site with a fascinating Bikepacker Radio archive and Lifestyle section

bikepacking.net - useful for bike set-up tips and equipment advice, including a handy readers' bikes section

adventurecycling.org - the home of Adventure Cyclist magazine and the Adventure Cycling Association, featuring an Open Road Gallery of readers' adventures

backcountrybiking.co.uk - a unusual UK site that combines bikepacking and packrafting, with skills courses, blogs and bespoke adventures

ROUTE-FINDING SITES

mtbroutefinder.co.uk - an exhaustive supply of UK off-road routes, easy to filter by difficulty and including Rough Ride Guides' published routes

mtbtrails.info - a huge selection of natural and 'epic' trails, particularly in the north of England and Scotland, with a detailed search engine to find just the ride you are after

forestry.gov.uk / scotland.forestry.gov.uk - details of mountain bike routes through English and Scottish Forestry Commission land

singletrackworld.com (Singletrack Magazine) - what this resource lacks in quantity, it more than makes up for in quality, with detailed information and pictures of every trail

mbr.co.uk/routes (MBR Magazine) - a fantastic site, with a section on 'Britain's best remote trails' and downloadable gps files

bikeradar.com/forums (What Mountain Bike and MBUK Magazines) - a great place for discussing proposed routes with riders who know them

plotaroute.com - contributor-led resource with thousands of routes and their profiles. Just select an area, click 'off-road' and away you go!

mapmyride.com - while these routes, created solely by MapMyRide app users, can vary tremendously, the easy-to-use search engine is great for inspiration

Downloadable maps and GPX files for the routes in this book are provided online and can be found using the last two words of the relevant chapter e.g. the first chapter is at *www.wildthingspublishing.com /bikepacking/ofsalisbury*

EPIC WILDERNESS RIDES

WHERE THE WILD THINGS ARE

Perhaps bikepacking's biggest USP (if it needed one) is the opportunity it gives for self-supported sojourns into the unknown. Surely there can be no greater feeling of adventure for a cyclist than traversing the wildest, most untameable of places, far from civilisation. With careful planning, you'll be surprised how far into the wild a mountain bike can take you. Long distance paths such as the Pennine Way and Great Glen Way can be fantastic expeditions to undertake by mountain bike, or if you're a little more pushed for time one of these rides will give you a fix of unadulterated wilderness:

RIDE 24: A ROOM WITH A VIEW

With no living soul save for the Glenforsa estate manager within 8km of the Tomsleibhe bothy, a night in this wonderful glen on Mull is one of the remotest imaginable. Surrounded by silent, insurmountable hills on all sides, the only way in or out of the glen is on an estate road which, by the time it reaches the bothy, is little more than a sliver of trail. The soundtrack to your stay here will just be the howling wind, the flow of the river below you and the occasional cry of an eagle. An overnight stay doesn't get much more wild than this.

RIDE 7: A TASTE OF THE TORS

Though on the north-eastern fringe of the National Park and only a dozen kilometres from the town of Moretonhampstead, the barren moors that spread west from Lustleigh have a particularly remote, isolated feel to them. The moor tops around Grimspound, scattered with gorse, scrub and granite crags are a navigational nightmare, and in inclement conditions really live up to their name, but in fairer weather this corner of Dartmoor is barren in the most beautiful of ways.

RIDES 29 & 30: TRANS-WALES NORTH AND SOUTH

The epic nature of this pair of rides, which together span Wales from the north to the south coast, only reinforces the feeling of an expedition through the wilderness. Though never straying too far from Offa's Dyke, and hence the English border, it does however traverse some wild places indeed. From the Clwydian Range and the Berwyn Hills to the Black Mountains and Brecon Beacons, the route exposes you to some truly remote terrain, particularly the huge crevice of Harley Dingle near Radnor Forest.

TECHNICAL TRAILS
FOR THE SINGLETRACK-MINDED

Many bikepackers are mountain bikers at heart, pure and simple. Trail rides are often defined, and certainly remembered, by technical singletrack sections that test your nerve and handling skills, and beg to be tackled at full speed. This is often where trail centres come into their own, with man-made trails built for just such a thrill, but the natural world has its own way of providing sublime singletrack – the movement of wild animals and people over time having created long, narrow paths of least resistance across the land, many of which are a match for your favourite black run.

RIDE 13: SANCTUARY ON THE SOLENT
Brighstone Forest forms the cornerstone of this ride, and is its undoubted highlight, with tight, twisting wooded singletrack emanating from the main trails like veins. Off-camber roots and natural berms make some of the tracks real technical challenges, while the flowing paths of the Tennyson Trail heading east towards Carisbrooke are too tempting to tackle at anything less than full pelt.

RIDE 19: RIDING ON THE EDGE
Though punctuated by flat reservoir trails and roads, there is some thrilling singletrack in this part of the Dark Peaks, home to some of the finest trail riding in England. The narrow, slippery stone setts leading off Derwent Edge call for sharp handling skills, but later descents can be taken at full throttle, leaning the bike round switchback turns before embracing gravity with abandon.

RIDE 21: HIGH HILLS, DEEP DALES
The fact that Fremington is home to the Dales Bike Centre tells you something about the quality of the trails in this corner of the Dales. Set among sweeping hills, much of the route is on firm, flowing, open trails with plenty of room to manoeuvre. If you like it tight and technical though, then Fremington Edge and the old mine workings over Whiteside Moor won't disappoint.

FAMILY RIDES

BETTER TOGETHER

Wild camping and back-country riding may not seem ideally suited to younger kids, but with a little planning and careful selection of trail and ride length, children can have an absolute blast, and they'll be planning their next adventure before you have even finished. I started by introducing my sons to simple forest tracks, with prefabricated tents and other ready-made camping options waiting for them at the end of the day. There's no reason why glamping shouldn't have a place where bikepacking is concerned, particularly when riding with kids. It takes away a little of the uncertainty and it won't be long before they are itching to join you in a den of your own making. The lure of camping pods, yurts and berber tents or even gipsy caravans can work wonders to get children to join you, and as long as the riding isn't overly taxing and you finish by toasting marshmallows or something equally delicious over an open fire, any doubts they may have will soon melt away. After all, what child doesn't love a good adventure?

RIDE 23: TAMING THE WILDS OF WINDERMERE

With low-level trails stretching between Grizedale Forest and Lake Windermere, not to mention a wealth of waymarked Forestry Commission options, this route packs a lot into a short distance. Forest singletrack and lake-side trails abound, children will love the camping options at the National Trust's Low Wray campsite and there's a magical castle just a stone's throw from their bed for the night. What more could they want?

RIDE 2: AVON CALLING

With a number of refreshment stops and bail-out options en route, and an enchanting ride through two eerily lit tunnels, this ride will be a sure-fire winner with children of all ages. There are plenty of distractions in Bath, and wooden dens scattered throughout Rainbow Wood. The ride also gets easier as it goes on, with a beautiful towpath stretch through the Avon Valley should you choose to ride the whole way to Avoncliff.

RIDE 9: LONDON'S GREENEST GATEWAY

Although I rode this route with grown-up company, I couldn't help but feel it would have been great with my boys. Beautifully flat, flowing forest singletrack runs across its entire length, and though following this route as far as Cheshunt may be too far for some little legs, there are a number of stations close by should you chose to quit while you're ahead. A proper forest camp in full view of London's flickering lights should leave them spellbound.

COASTAL TRAILS
FROM SEA TO SHINING SEA

There's nothing like the vast expanse of ocean to signify the end of a fulfilling journey – long-distance paths such as the Wessex Ridgeway and the Shipwrights Way, which end at Lyme Regis and Portsmouth respectively, are testament to that. So too is the fascination of many a cyclist with the coast-to-coast ride, a spectacular off-road version from Bonnar Bridge to Ullapool being my favourite. With some 31,000km of coastline around Great Britain it's never too difficult to incorporate coastal trails or sea views into an adventure ride. And there's nothing more satisfying than camping among the sand-dunes, being lulled to sleep by the rhythm of the waves.

RIDE 5: JURASSIC ROLLER COASTER
The pebbly beaches and sandy coves along Sidmouth's seafront give plenty of opportunity to camp above the high tide mark, but leaving you close enough to smell the sea as you fall asleep. The Jurassic Coast will be your companion for much of the ride too, and is visible from Harcombe Hill all the way to Mutter's Moor and Bulverton Hill.

RIDE 6: VALLEY OF THE ROCKS – AN EXMOOR EPIC
Dramatic coastal views grace much of the northern section of this route from Simonsbath. As soon as you drop down from Cherrybridge, the Valley of the Rocks unfurls before you. From Lee Abbey it's worth walking round the South West Coast Path into Lynmouth just to expose yourself to the jagged, wind-swept drama of it all. Just hope the sea breeze helps push you up the hellishly steep road climb that follows.

RIDE 4: A STUDLAND SORTIE
It's rare to find bridleway that skirts so close to the edge of sea cliffs – paths close to such precipices tend to be footpaths. However, the Purbecks ride will take you right to the brink of Old Harry Rocks, the white needle-like cliffs at the end of Studland Bay. You'll be treated to a glorious coastal panorama all the way from Ridgeway Hill to Ferry Road and will be spoiled for choice with wild camps with a sea view too – Swyre Head perhaps having the best views of all.

WINTER RIDES
RIDING IN A WINTER WONDERLAND

Many are those who pack up their bikes for the winter, or turn to their cross-bike for short local loops when conditions allow, but with some sensible additions to your kit bag, there's no reason not to carry on bikepacking right through the year. With enough insulating layers, plenty of hot drinks and a small fire to bed down with, you can immerse yourself in scenery lent that magical frosty sheen, when to less hardy souls these perfectly pristine-looking landscapes remain tantalisingly out of bounds.

RIDE 16: A DRIFT THROUGH WILD MIDLAND MEADOWS
The often hard-packed, well-paved and occasionally metalled trails along the Peddars Way make it a rideable route all through the year. Though Thetford Forest may get a little sticky in the wet, it seemed to drain surprisingly well after numerous April showers when I rode it. A fairly flat route throughout, it should let you keep up a good pace should you need to keep warm too.

RIDE 10: FINDING EFRAFA
The Wayfarers Walk, which forms the backbone of this ride, crosses chalky downs on its way to the warrens of Watership Down. Though sometimes slippery, the route drains pretty well, and there are enough hard-packed sections to make the occasional wooded segments easier to bear, should the ground be sodden. There's plenty of shelter to be found on the downs too, if you need to escape an icy wind.

RIDE 8: A GREEN RIBBON THROUGH THE BIG SMOKE
There's something quite special about riding off-road through London in frost, ice or snow. While the rest of the traffic moves tentatively around or grinds to a halt altogether, you can leave it all behind and strike out across crisp white fields that crunch beneath your wheels. If it's really too cold to brave an alfresco night on a common, there are plenty of accommodation options on tap, but if you can cope with the chill it really is worth making the most of being the only soul on the entire park or common – a rarity in such a crowded city.

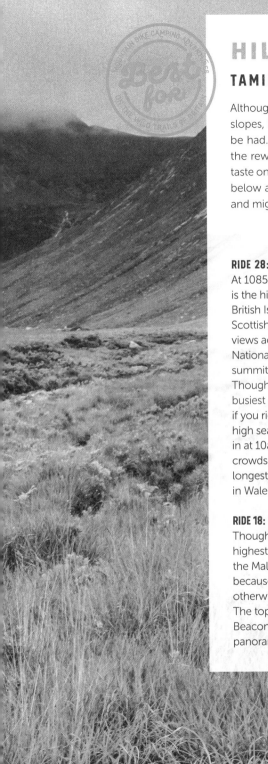

HILLS AND MOUNTAINS
TAMING THE TORS

Although it's tempting to steer a laden bike away from the steeper slopes, it's here where the most memorable experiences are to be had. It is worth grinding or pushing up gruelling climbs for the rewards you'll reach at the summit, as well as those you'll taste on the way back down. The views I experienced on the rides below are still etched in my mind, long after leaving these high and mighty wild places behind.

RIDE 28: TOUCHING THE SKY
At 1085m, Mount Snowdon is the highest point in the British Isles outside the Scottish Highlands, and the views across the Snowdonia National Park from the summit are second to none. Though described as 'the busiest mountain in Britain', if you ride up before the high season curfew kicks in at 10am you'll miss the crowds and have one of the longest mountain descents in Wales all to yourself.

RIDE 18: MALVERN'S GREAT SENTINEL
Though by no means the highest ride I have chosen, the Malverns are memorable because they dominate an otherwise flat landscape. The top of Worcestershire Beacon affords a spectacular panorama over Herefordshire, Gloucestershire, the Severn Valley, Welsh mountains and the Bristol Channel, not to mention the spires of Worcester, Gloucester and Hereford cathedrals. What a view to wake up to after a wild camp at the summit!

RIDE 22: RISING TO THE CHALLENGE
Buttermere is such a bucolic name, yet the routes that connect the lake here to Ennerdale are brutal. Scree-scattered slopes and occasional quagmires make already demanding gradients unrideable at times. But even hiking your bike on your shoulders at times is a small price to pay for the breathtaking views throughout this ride. Gazing out over Whiteless Pike, Knott Rigg and Hindscarth, you really can feel like the king of all you survey.

THE SOUTH WEST

THE DEVERILLS IN THE DETAIL

WILTSHIRE'S WYLYE VALLEY AND DEVERILL HILLS MAKE FOR AN EPIC MICRO-ADVENTURE

The barren plateau of Salisbury Plain dominates my neighbouring county of Wiltshire. I have ridden here many times but often yearned for a more interesting off-road route. This county does harbour some stunning sections of bridleway and old drovers' roads, particularly along the Cranborne Chase and West Wiltshire Downs Area of Outstanding Natural Beauty, but they seemed too fragmented, or too far from any railway line to make a viable point-to-point adventure ride. Until, that is, after hours spent poring over maps I managed to link

the fabulous riding to be found among the Deverills to the south of Warminster with the stunning Wylye Valley, a Roman road cutting through the Great Ridge Woods and a segment of the Monarch's Way long-distance path. Finishing the ride on the edge of Longleat forest would then leave just a few miles to either Warminster or Westbury stations, or Frome for that matter, just over the county border in Somerset.

Tisbury is a lovely little village steeped in history. With evidence of a Bronze Age settlement and possibly a 4,000-year-old henge monument, Tisbury

---

INFO:

START: Tisbury station, Station Road SP3 6JT, 51.060689, -2.078945
FINISH: The Bath Arms, Horningsham BA12 7LY, 51.174110, -2.273493

DISTANCE: 21.9 miles/35.3km   **ASCENT:** 2578ft/786m   **OFF-ROAD:** 80%

TERRAIN: Stone, chalk, grass and dirt bridleways and byways, with occasional country lanes.

PUBLIC TRANSPORT: This ride finishes at Horningsham, which is just a few miles from Warminster, Westbury or Frome stations.

NAVIGATION: Tricky in places. Although all the rights of way are signposted, sometimes it is hard to follow them, particularly on the descent to Brixton Deverill. It's also difficult heading towards Sherrington where, turning left on a bridleway through Park Bottom, you should ride up the grassy bank to the right to locate the path rather than ride across the valley floor, where the path eventually peters out. OS Landranger 118 and 143 could be useful.

EAT AND DRINK:

Tisbury Delicatessen, High St, Tisbury, Salisbury SP3 6HA, 01747 871771
The George Inn, Longbridge Deverill, Wiltshire BA12 7DG, 01985 840396, www.the-georgeinn.co.uk

SLEEP:

The Dove Inn, Corton, Warminster, BA12 0SZ, 01985 850109, www.thedove.co.uk
Botany Camping & Glamping, Botany Farm, Bradley Rd, Warminster BA12 7JY, 07713 404233, www.botanycamping.com
Bivvy: Boyton Down

PROVISIONS:

Pythouse Kitchen Garden, Café & Shop, West Hatch, Tisbury, Wiltshire SP3 6PA, 01747 870444, www.pythousekitchengarden.co.uk
Bachelors Bikes, Warminster, Wiltshire, 07920 510811, www.bikz.co.uk

prospered during the 13th century as its quarries provided the stone for Salisbury Cathedral's construction. Before I set off on the trail I first sought out the village's 15th century tithe barn to marvel at what is the largest thatched roof in England. I also noted the giant yew tree in the parish churchyard, thought to be some 4,000 years old and the second oldest in Britain.

The village's fantastic little deli was my last stop before I climbed on the bike in earnest and started up a dragging road climb through the village, before peeling off up a quiet lane, gardens on either side bathed in sunshine, their residents enjoying leisurely al fresco lunches. As I trundled out along a flat dirt path I could see new houses rising beyond the cornfields, a testament to this pretty village's growing popularity with London commuters.

I was disappointed that there was no public right of way through Fonthill Abbey Wood from this side, as I would have been interested to see what little is left of the 'abbey', actually a Gothic revival country house, the tower of which repeatedly collapsed, eventually necessitating its demolition. Still, if I could have got through the Fonthill estate, I would have accidentally bypassed the Great Ridge which turned out to be one of highlights of the journey. I had looked forward to a swim in Fonthill Lake, especially with the temperature slowly rising throughout that morning, but as I rode past the 2km-long stretch of water I realised that the thin tendrils that made their way through the silt would offer no such opportunity.

Instead I pressed on, past the village of Fonthill Bishop and up onto the downs, the rumble from the A303 fading away as I climbed towards the treeline of Great Ridge, the only expanse of woodland between here and my journey's end in Longleat Forest. The Deverills were almost entirely exposed, offering no shelter to the would-be wild camper. That I hoped to find in the small copses that overlook the Wylye Valley, but for now I headed along the shrouded ridgeline to the downs, its arrow-straight course testament to its Roman legacy. The dappled shade along Great Ridge offered some much-needed respite from the afternoon heat, and as I headed deeper into the woods I started to pick out a network of trails heading out in all directions.

The ground fell sharply away to the north east, and an intriguing footpath went with it, but my focal point was due north to the middle of the Wylye Valley and the promise of refreshment at Corton. The Wessex Ridgeway path (there is a long distance path of the same name over the border in Dorset, though unconnected) guided me out of the trees to a crossroads of wide, dusty paths. Ahead wound a trail down the valley slope towards Boyton, where small copses promised shelter and fine views over the Wylye River, which I noted for later.

My path ran north-west past grazing pasture, a wildflower-lined avenue that took two kilometres to drop lazily to the valley road. It was here that I stumbled upon the lovely Dove Inn at Corton, where I lingered awhile outside, feeling the early evening air beginning to cool. As those in search of supper began flocking to its indoor tables I dug my down jacket out from the bottom of my bag, having thought that it would be surplus to requirements given the temperature earlier in the day, before heading back up the trail to the camping spot I'd noticed earlier, the curiously named North Soupir copse (*soupir*, as far as I could ascertain, is French for 'sigh' or for a quarter note musical rest).

I was glad to find that at last the ground and vegetation was dry enough for firewood, and it was not long before I had a small campfire crackling away. I always find a camp fire transforms my experience of wild camping. It becomes less about hunkering down, staying insulated and trying to find comfort to get you through the night, and more about savouring the experience, luxuriating in its warmth,

appreciating all the more the wonder of your sur-roundings as dusk turns to darkness. I ringed my small fire pit with stones and cleared all other dry debris well away, so I could let the fire die down gradually as I started to slumber. I needn't have sought shelter that evening; the sky was so clear and calm that there was little chance of rain. However, I allowed myself the luxury of leaving the tarp in my bag and from the edge of the trees, as the sun sank behind the Deverills, I sleepily picked out the first stars in the deep blue above Salisbury Plain and stretched out by the dying embers to sleep.

I awoke to an overcast sky and loitered only long enough to bury the ashes from my fire and cook two cupfuls of porridge, realising there might not be anywhere to get supplies until I reached the Somerset border. Slinging my dry-bags back onto the bike I retraced my tyre tracks to the valley road at Corton for a brief tarmac stretch to warm up, before the morning's impending climb. The road snaked through Tytherington, another of the valley's idyllic thatched villages, in an 'S' bend where the trail doubled back and then turned and ramped up Tytherington Hill.

From up here I could trace the line of the Roman road I had briefly joined on the Great Ridge, as it continued faintly but unerringly toward Monkton Deverill. I was heading to another of the five Deverills – not Longbridge, Hill or Kingston, but Brixton Deverill, beyond which the toughest climb of my journey awaited, so I was glad just to keep the height I had already gained as I took in the surpris-ingly arid-looking panorama. It wasn't long though before I had to drop down off Summerslade Down, before the trail turned too far south-west, and as I passed the parish church, which rubbed shoulders with the gardens of a fine-looking country house, I was greeted by two other mountain bikers – both local, it turned out – who went on to extol the many

virtues of off-road riding in the Deverills. From my ride thus far I couldn't help but agree but I was unaware at this point that the best was yet to come.

They wished me good luck on the climb up to the desolate sounding Cold Kitchen Hill, but it was not fortune I needed up this hellishly steep climb, but an extra pair of legs – or better still, a motor. Bereft of both, however, I made do with what I had, and settled into a torturously slow rhythm, zig-zagging from side to side in a futile bid to mitigate the gradient. At what seemed like the crest of the hill, a glorious view unfolded – the best of these, I've found, are always hard won by bike. The hill arced round in the shape of a huge crescent, dwarfing the tiny farms that lay in its basin, and the trail, now just a faint grassy bridle path, followed the shape of the hill, climbing gradually all the way past Cold Kitchen Hill's lofty trig point at 257 metres. From here the conifers of Longleat were clearly visible, and each pedal stroke appeared to bring them closer still.

The ridgeline must be more than 5km long, giving plenty of time to take in the views. The top of Brimsdown Hill, at the far end of the crescent, must be the highest point for miles, eclipsing by almost 50 metres the likes of Cley Hill on the other side of Longleat. Although hard won, the height was easily lost, though technical trails and overgrown bridle-ways slowed my progress off the slope somewhat. At the bottom, though, I had lost 100 metres in just over half a kilometre. From here it was wide grassy bridleways worn down by farm traffic before an undulating road stretch carried me to Horning-sham and the wonderful Bath Arms, where the staff happily pack a lunch for their guests to take on their explorations of Longleat and beyond – which was exactly what I intended to do. I was immensely glad on this journey to have discovered that there is nothing 'plain' about off-road adventuring south of Salisbury.

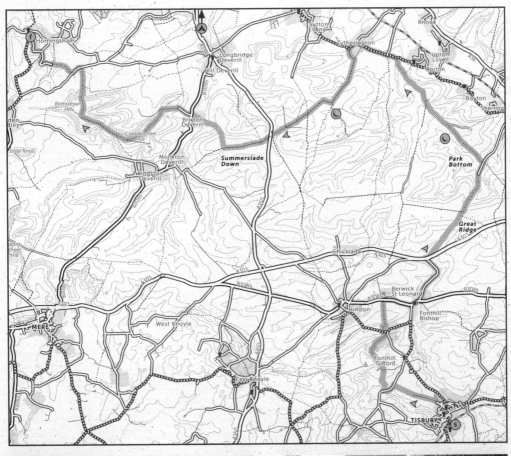

51

AVON CALLING

A SCENIC CROSS-COUNTRY ROUTE THAT MEANDERS FROM A SOMERSET MARKET TOWN TO THE HEART OF BATH, AND OUT ALONG THE AVON VALLEY

I have lived in this neck of the woods for over a decade now, spending much of that time commuting by bike from Frome to Bath's unique Roman baths and thermal spas that flow at its heart. Only recently, though, have I discovered a beautiful off-road route to connect both scenic cycle options into its centre – Sustrans' new Two Tunnels Greenway through the hills from Midford, and the Kennet and Avon Canal towpath, which winds its way into Bath along the breathtakingly beautiful Avon Valley to the south east. How frustrating to know that for 10 years I had needlessly

cycled treacherous stretches of B-road to get to either of these green city gateways!

Eager to try this newly mapped-out journey, my three kids and I set out one Saturday morning, with all the time in the world to make a leisurely loop from our market town in Somerset via the city of Bath to the Wiltshire border, where we could catch a train home the following day, after camping out in the Bath hills. We set off in a small convoy, laden with all our camping kit, and began our journey along a Sustrans route that followed deserted narrow lanes out of town to familiar

INFO:

START: Frome station, Station Approach, Wallbridge BA11 1RE, 51.227314, -2.309997
FINISH: Avoncliff station BA15 2HD, 51.339576, -2.281899

DISTANCE: 27.6 miles/44.5km **ASCENT:** 3133ft/955m **OFF-ROAD:** 65%

TERRAIN: Dirt bridle track, quiet byways and lanes, traffic-free tarmac through the Greenway, and stony tow path. Moderate climbs get steeper around Bath, with a flat towpath to the end.

NAVIGATION: Easy. With quiet road sections, signed bridle paths and NCN 24 waymarks, this route shouldn't present any problems. On the wooded descent north of Faulkland take an unsigned right at a crossroads; a little further on, along the bridleway to Wellow, as you climb keep the hedgerow on your left and don't descend until you have passed the Long Barrow mound on your left. OS Landranger maps 142 and 155 cover all but the final canal section.

EAT AND DRINK:

The Talbot, Selwood Street, Mells, Frome, Somerset BA11 3PN, 01373 812254, www.talbotinn.com

Cross Guns, Avoncliff, Bradford-on-Avon, Wiltshire BA15 2HB, 01225 862335, www.crossguns.net

SLEEP:

The Castle Inn, Mount Pleasant, Bradford-on-Avon, Wiltshire BA15 1SJ, 01225 865657, www.flatcappers.co.uk

Pitchperfect, Woolverton, Somerset BA2 7QU, 01373 830733, www.pitchperfectcamping.co.uk

Bivvy: Claverton Down

PROVISIONS:

The Walled Garden, Selwood Street, Mells, Somerset BA11 3PN, 01373 812597, www.thewalledgardenatmells.co.uk

Cycology, The Old Courthouse, Waterloo, Frome BA11 3FE, 01373 469590, www.cycologybikes.co.uk

haunts down by the river at Vallis Woods, where youngsters had created their own pump track among the trees. We had eyes for something other than berms and jumps today, though, so rode on to a bridge where the shallow river widens at Great Elm – another spot where the boys have spent hours building boats, fishing for crays or swinging precariously out over the water on rope swings. There's the first in a series of lovely stretches of singletrack here, set far back from, but running parallel with the Mells road, scything through the moss-covered buildings of ancient quarry works, the path strewn with globules of iron ore.

Our first port of call was the picturesque village of Mells, where a walled garden hides a botanical nursery, café and outdoor pizza parlour's wood-fired oven. Were it a little later in the day we'd have opted for a pizza here, or a drink in the cobbled courtyard of the splendid Talbot pub over the road. Instead the boys chose the café's rich hot chocolate, before we continued on our way, back on quiet lanes to where the waymarked route drops down to the path of an old railway line.

However, today we would be ploughing our own furrow, and we continued on to the farmsteads of Hardington Mandeville, where a bridle path led us through one field of grazing cattle, then another, where we followed a thin path trampled through waist-high grasses. At times my youngest lad was almost lost from sight, but the constant chatter between siblings was enough to let me know he was still with us. As we emerged from the grasses round the side of a farm we sent a menagerie of ducks, geese and quail scattering from beneath our wheels.

On through Hemington to Faulkland, where legendary cider house Tucker's Grave called last orders purportedly for the last time a few years ago, only for the landlady of 40 years, Glenda, to realise her mistake and reopen her tiny tap room to the relief of many a loyal customer. The interior of this iconic Somerset pub has remained unaltered throughout its 200-year history, and though there's considerable conjecture about the name Tucker's Grave, there's little doubt it inspired The Stranglers, who have been known to sup scrumpy here, and wrote a song of the same name for their 2004 album *Norfolk Coast*.

As we headed out across golden brown hills, a rutted byway got progressively muddier as it dropped into a wooded valley, but the heavy going barely bothered the boys – they were having far too much fun skidding down this slippery slope with back wheels locked up. With shins caked in mud we emerged from the trees, riding round the edges of fields ripe with corn. The brow of an ancient long barrow site protruded from the far reaches of one field, and soon we were back on firmer ground and careening, brakes squealing, to splash through the ford at Wellow, where we re-joined the NCN route into Bath.

Instead of following its signs to the old railway path, now sanitised and gravelled, and which leads to Wellow's trekking centre and café, we found a parallel byway, overgrown with bramble and almost hidden from view, which took us most of the way to Midford. It's here that steep hills rise to surround Bath, and where in 1874 the Somerset and Dorset Joint Railway tunnelled beneath Combe Down to connect Midford to Bath's Green Park station. At over a mile long Combe Down tunnel was the UK's longest without intermediate ventilation and now, as part of the Two Tunnels Greenway project which opened in 2013, is the longest cycling tunnel in Britain.

The boys loved the surreal, spot-lit interlude of both Combe Down and the shorter Devon-shire tunnel, made all the more so by the classical soundtrack being piped along the old railway line

as well as the whoops and hollers of other equally excited kids echoing from far ahead. The Devonshire tunnel brought us out to Bear Flat, a plateau just above the city, where we grabbed paninis from a bijou Italian deli before heading into the city for that evening's surprise entertainment. We'd timed our journey into Bath to coincide with a televised criterium road race, which would take place around Victoria Park and Bath's emblematic Royal Crescent. Before long we were locking our bikes to crash barriers along the race route to join the throngs cheering as klaxons signalled the start of the main event. For an hour the boys watched, entranced by their first taste of professional circuit racing and gleefully ringing cowbells each time the riders sped past them; even I had to admit the park's tree-lined avenues made for the most memorable of velodromes. As the sun dipped low over the trees we milled about in the crowds awaiting the podium presentations, then took to our own bikes in search of the bridle paths that would take us to our camp for the night.

It was a steep climb past the university's campus, and I joined the boys pushing and puffing their way up the slope, but what better time to reach a vantage point over this beautiful city than as the sun started to lend a golden tinge to the city's pale limestone walls? We reached Bath's Rainbow Wood with just enough light left in the sky to fumble our way – still pushing – to a spot among the beeches near the Bath 'skyline' walk. By now the views down into Prior Park had all but vanished, but we would relish those in the morning; I had to deliver on my promise of campfire-cooked bangers and marshmallow-topped hot chocolates.

It was a deeply satisfying feeling being there, with my three boys looking weary but thrilled by their achievements. It was great to see them having a whale of a time on their bikes, in the open air, the lure of ever-present digital screens forgotten for the

day. The next day we would head down to the dry, dusty towpath along the Kennet and Avon canal for a morning of flat riding – for which the boys would be grateful. We'd stop for ice creams along the way and maybe take a dip in the river near Bradford-on-Avon if we made it that far (both Freshford and nearby Avoncliff have stops on the railway line that follows the route of both river and canal).

Camping out, we enjoyed each other's company, unfettered by routines, timetables or homework. I could tell from the boys' contented faces that we didn't do these off-the-cuff adventures enough, and resolved to rectify that in future. Munching piping-hot sausages stuffed into the last of our deli bread, the boys asked for stories until they were too tired to listen any more. Beyond Prior Park the city was aglow, but a hush had descended on our woods along with the darkness – the only sounds I could hear were the soft breathing of tired but happy children who would remember this little adventure for years to come.

It may have been close to home, but I hoped our night beneath the stars in Rainbow Wood would inspire them to go in search of their own adventures, and as a father I'm beginning to realise that's exactly what they'll do one day, and sooner than I imagine, so our time together now becomes all the more precious.

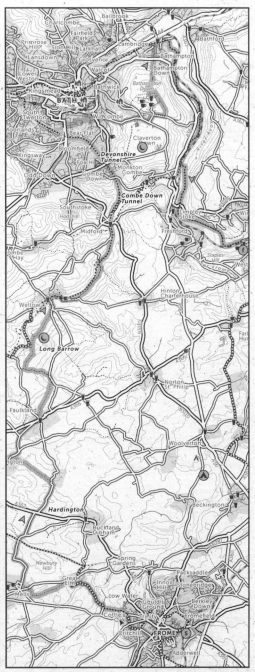

CRESTING THE QUANTOCKS

A BIKEPACKER'S PARADISE AND MICROCOSM OF BRITISH MOUNTAIN BIKING, THE QUANTOCKS ARE PACKED WITH WOODED CLIMBS, SWEEPING DESCENTS AND WONDERFUL RIDGELINE VIEWS

If you could distil cross-country mountain biking into its purest form, the result would bear an uncanny resemblance to the Quantocks. A diminutive range of hills along the west Somerset coast, they span no more than a dozen or so kilometres, but with a multitude of combes tumbling down off Great Ridge, which forms the range's spine, there is a wealth of riding potential here. The Quantocks contain more bridleways per kilometre than anywhere else in the country. In truth the hills stretch from West Quantoxhead near the Bristol Channel some 24km down towards the Vale of

Taunton Deane, but the best riding is to be had along a 10km strip between its north-western tip and Aisholt Common on the edge of Great Wood.

While the ridge barely rises beyond about 350 metres, there is a surprising amount of climbing and descending on a Quantocks ride. If you are not cruising across the ridge, the chances are you'll be flying flat out down stony singletrack or through natural sandy berms, splashing through streams in the lower combes or climbing on technical rock gardens. Whenever I come here I think of this place as a natural trail centre, capturing the essence of

INFO:

START / FINISH: Car park at Holford TA5 1SA, 51.162554, -3.211318

DISTANCE: 27.4 miles/44.1km   **ASCENT:** 4133ft/1260m   **OFF-ROAD:** 80%

TERRAIN: Stony wooded gullies, wide grassy bridleways along the ridge and dirt singletrack through Great Wood. Climbing up the combes tends to be short and sharp; the ridge isn't flat but the climbs are more drawn out.

NAVIGATION: Straightforward. Despite the multitude of bridleways packed into the Quantocks there are very few that aren't signposted, and the hills' compact nature means getting your bearings is never too difficult. OS Landranger 181 can be useful though.

EAT AND DRINK:

The Bicknoller Inn, 32 Church Lane, Bicknoller, Somerset TA4 4EL, 01984 656234, www.bicknollerinn.com
The Plough Inn, Holford, Somerset TA5 1RY, 01278 741652

SLEEP:

The Hood Arms, Kilve, Somerset TA5 1EA, 01278 741210, www.thehoodarms.com
Moorhouse Campsite, Holford, Bridgwater, Somerset TA5 1SP, 01278 741295, www.moorhousecampsite.co.uk
Bivvy: Round Hill in Great Wood nr Plainsfield

PROVISIONS:

Cricketer Farm Shop & Cafe, Stowey Court Farm, Nether Stowey, Somerset TA5 1LL, 01278 732207, www.cricketershop.co.uk
St John Street Cycles, 91-93 St John Street, Bridgwater, Somerset TA6 5HX, 01278 441500, www.sjscycles.co.uk

British trail biking in a short rollercoaster ride in the west Somerset hills. It never fails to surprise me how quickly dense, wooded gullies dissolve into open heathland flecked with yellow and purple heather, or how suddenly the arduous combe climbs give way to far-reaching views across the channel and to Wales.

It was from Holford village that a friend and I made the ascent of Hodder's Combe to experience just these sudden transitions. Already a spider's web of singletrack had opened up before us; so too a surprisingly expansive vista after so brief a climb. Smith's Combe's rocky cascade dropped away before us revealing a panoramic coastal view spanning from Minehead's sandy bay in the west, past the ominous silhouette of Hinkley Point power station to vast stretches of mudflats along Burnham-on-Sea to the east. And beyond them, below a broiling mass of clouds, the distant Vale of Glamorgan rose across the Channel.

Angular columns of heavy rain interspersed by rare rays of weak sunshine lent the scene a touch of drama, and it was with the distant roll of thunder in our ears that we pressed on, soon hurtling down Pardlestone Hill to join the Coleridge Way, a long-distance path that used to run from nearby Nether Stowey to Porlock, until a recent extension took it on to Lynmouth. Now covering 80 rideable kilometres, it traverses the Quantocks, the Brendan Hills and Exmoor: the unmistakable Somerset landscape that inspired the poetry of Samuel Taylor Coleridge and William Wordsworth. Together they penned their *Lyrical Ballads*, a key work in the English Romantic movement, while living at the foot of the Quantocks.

After picking our way back up the rock garden of Smith's Combe, a succession of squat hills – Beacon, Black Ball and Thorncombe – ushered us into a fittingly poetic scene. Across Great Ridge we watched black clouds tumble across the coast while the western flank of the Quantocks was bathed in a pale wash of afternoon sunshine – a riot of pastel colours on one side, stark monochromes on the other. With glorious singletrack stretching out invitingly across the open heath, which rolls in waves beyond Hurley Beacon towards the highest point on the hills – Will's Neck, beyond Great Wood – the gathering storm was finally unleashed upon the hillside. We had no choice but to dive down Black Hill to sit out the storm, which lashed the canopy of Holford Combe. Ferocious lightning soon sent us scuttling down the stone-strewn combe to our van. We hadn't planned to drop down this descent until returning from a wild camp in Great Wood tomorrow, and under different circumstances we would have relished this long, flowing and challenging descent, but the storm pushed us unceremoniously off the heath.

To the soundtrack of thunder, not so much rumbling as booming overhead, we resigned ourselves to the fact that our ride for the day was over. The electrical storm raged on, lighting crackling across the leaden sky, so we rustled up supper on the camper's stove, before somewhat despondently seeking out the village pub. Discussion at the bar was dominated by talk of the apocalyptic weather, but despite the disappointment, retreating to our starting

point to lick our wounds was the only sensible option. Our VW camper was our 'plan B', and this time I'd been glad we had one.

Once the storm had passed, a harvest moon lent a soft glow to the wooded embankment behind the village. We decided to seize our opportunity, so finished our drinks, rolled our bikes out of the van and remounted to climb the technical tunnel of Holford Combe. We barely needed our nightlights as the moonlight flooded in through the trees to illuminate our path. Our night-time passage up onto the ridge was an altogether different experience to that before the storm. The air was still and fresh, and, besides our wheels whipping across sodden terrain, all else was silent. Seeing the villages below us on either side lit up like a runway kept us on track along the crest, and amid the darkness they made us feel almost thrust into the heavens.

Along Will's Neck to Middle Hill then Lydeard Hill we made rapid progress. We were closer to the south-west edge of the Quantocks now, the escarpment falling quickly away from Will's Neck down the steep banks of Bagborough Hill. Beyond that on the road through Bicknoller and Flaxpool we could trace the movement of traffic, the iridescent glow of car headlights looking for all the world like a procession of fireflies. At this hour, though, the lines of the West Somerset steam railway beyond lay dormant.

The drop down over 100 metres to Gib Hill was unexpected, and the chill breeze on the descent briefly knocked the wind from us. Eager to make hay while the moon shone, we tackled the descent and our subsequent passage to the ride's furthest point – Enmore – at the same pace we would have travelled in daylight, rocketing through the last of the woods and out onto slippery country lanes. We were soon eating into our return leg from the Vale of Taunton Deane – though by now it was almost midnight. When at last we did tire, perhaps more due to the

pace than the distance, it was close to the banks of Hawkridge Reservoir, up on Round Hill near Plainsfield. It was a beautiful view across the water's mirror-like surface and over the silent plains rolling out to the Bristol Channel, and we were so thrilled to be out there we soaked it all up until the small hours. Under a simple tarp shelter we grabbed a few hours shut eye and were up at the crack of dawn keen to press home the advantage of clear skies.

After a breakfast of stewed apple and porridge we packed up and dove into Great Wood with the same abandon as yesterday, happy to jump from one combe to the next, grinding up one then barrelling down the next, covering twice as much distance as we needed to, and eventually leaving the treeline at Dead Woman's Ditch. Stories abound of how in 1789 local charcoal burner John Walford murdered his nagging wife here, yet maps dated from before the murder show this place already christened with its grizzly name.

We reined in the pace so as not to frighten ponies grazing in the half light on the raised plains of Great Bear before disappearing into tight, weaving single-track along the wooded upper banks of Dowsborough. Unsurprisingly the gulley of Holford Combe was familiar to us now, and as we picked our way through the stones for the third and final time we relished every centimetre of the 2km drop back to Holford.

For us it was a victory snatched from the jaws of defeat, an opportunity I was glad we'd grasped when it would have been all too easy to pack up and call it a night. In the end our evening out on the low hills of the Quantocks was little more than a pitstop, but when your window of opportunity could close at any moment, you don't want to sleep your way through it. Riding both day and night had wrung so much more out of these diminutive hills than we could have hoped for. Every cloud, it seems, has a silver lining.

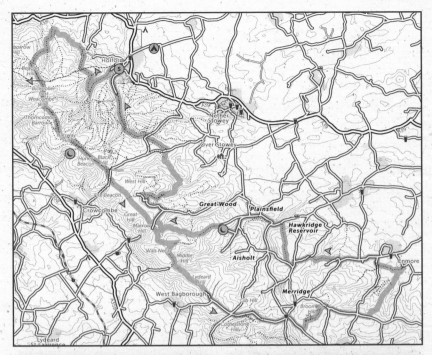

A STUDLAND SORTIE

DISCOVER THE ISLE OF PURBECK'S WEALTH OF RIDING, FROM PINE FORESTS TO CLIFFTOP TRAILS

Childhood memories came flooding back on my return to the Isle of Purbeck, of camping meadows, white cliffs and dusky coastal downland, but most of all of the magical ruins of Corfe Castle seen through the smoke of the Swanage Railway locomotive. Returning here, nothing seemed to have changed and the 'isles' still retain an air of simple beauty, untouched by urban development. My circular ride started in the pine forests of Rempstone Heath, as I left the forest behind, crossing the road down to Studland and instantly climbing a winding, hard-packed

bridleway up Brenscombe Hill to the isle's main ridge. It is this crest, which stretches west from Studland almost as far as Lulworth Cove, that gave the Purbecks its misleading epithet. Never an island as such, the coast here used to be cut off from the rest of the country because the ridge was overgrown and impassable – Corfe Castle guarded the only gateway.

Fortunately no longer the case, the white parallel paths up here offered a swooping railroad of a descent into Corfe along chalky downs invaded by scrub, and as I dropped down into the

---

INFO:

START/FINISH: National Trust and Bankes Arms car park, Manor Road, Studland BH19 3AU, 50.641745, -1.946943

DISTANCE: 27.3 miles/43.9km   **ASCENT:** 3129ft/954m   **OFF-ROAD:** 80%

TERRAIN: Wide chalky doubletrack, forest and wooded singletrack, some grass and tarmac sections. Climbs tend to be long rather than steep.

NAVIGATION: Occasionally tricky. At the end of the track up to Ridgeway Hill, make sure you go through a gate to your left before continuing west, with the fence on your right. Following NCN Route 2 through Rempstone Heath, you will come to a staggered junction of five paths; don't follow Route 2 straight on here but take the second trail on your left to head due south. OS Landranger 195 could be useful.

EAT AND DRINK:

The Scott Arms, West Street, Kingston, Wareham, Dorset BH20 5LH, 01929 480270, www.thescottarms.com
Joe's Cafe, South Beach, Studland, Dorset BH19 3AN

SLEEP:

Olivers of Corfe Castle, 5 West Street, Corfe Castle, Wareham, Dorset BH20 5HA, 01929 477111
Camp: East Creech Farm, Creech, Wareham, Dorset BH20 5AP, 01929 480519, www.eastcreechfarm.co.uk
Bivvy: Newton Heath or Smedmore Hill

PROVISIONS:

Corfe Castle Village Stores, 25 East Street, Corfe Castle, Dorset BH20 5EE, 01929 481292
Charlie the Bikemonger, 5 Queens Road, Swanage, Dorset BH19 2EQ, 01929 475833, www.charliethebikemonger.com

town I made out the chug and whistle of the steam engine which echoed through the valley. I rode up to the station hoping to catch a glimpse of the train and sure enough as I reached the platform I was confronted with an instantly recognisable view. Leaning the bike against the station fence I headed up the platform stairs to see the Pullman carriages and down at the far end the dark green locomotive, wheezing in a cloud of steam, began to depart. And there, in the background, the ruined stronghold of Corfe Castle rose through the smoke like some ancient sentinel, before being lost in the shroud as the engine pulled away.

I rolled on too, following the train's evaporating trail of steam on a parallel road, to its next call at Norden, before turning off past an old campsite haunt of our family's and along a trail that drifted gradually away from grazing pasture, beyond which the Purbeck range rises dramatically, into dense woodland. Inclement weather had dogged

me all morning, and I welcomed the thick canopy overhead as I tackled the wood's technical single-track. I was soon exposed to the elements once more and had a harsh road climb to tackle, which switched back on itself in an almost Alpine fashion.

Then I was off across an ancient byway, now some 200 metres up on the aptly named Ridgeway Hill, and was rewarded for my labours with a fine sea view that would be with me for most of that afternoon. The rain clouds had rolled sullenly away too and glimmers of sunshine began to set the sea sparkling. Along the ridgeway I noticed Grange Arch, an 18th century folly built by the then-owner of the magnificent Creech Grange below as a vantage point from which to marvel over his estate. This is the second highest point on the Purbecks (the trail soon took me to the highest, Swyre Head at 208m), but from Grange Arch I met a road and needed to swing about and drop into Steeple down a sketchy rock-strewn bridleway; otherwise I'd have been heading into MoD territory, through whose firing ranges there are no off-road rights of way.

Before long though I was grinding back up to a plateau that ran through cornfields and the village of Kimmeridge before ramping up once more, past a rusting metal gate daubed with the words 'Hell Bottom' to a place that was anything but hellish. From the trig point at Swyre Head the views were nothing short of spectacular. Though this knoll was barren, grassy and fenced in from estate land, there was a path allowing access to a concave slope that gradually flattened as it rolled to the coast. It may have little shelter, but what a perfect place for a wild camp! A patchwork of fields was dissected by a narrow country lane and a few scattered dwellings, apart from which the scene was almost unspoilt by human hand. Past Kimmeridge Bay, the coastal view unfurled to

Broad Bench, Worbarrow Bay and Lulworth Cove, with Weymouth and the Isle of Portland almost hovering on a faint watery horizon.

If it weren't for the early hour and my plans to camp with friends later, I'd have stayed put and drunk in the views until the sun set, but I had to drag myself away, safe in the knowledge that an equally compelling vista awaited me at Old Harry Rocks. Apart from losing sight of the coast for a while, the journey there captured the essence of Purbeck riding – wide, furrowed chalk trails along exposed downland or singletrack ribbons through wooded or bramble-strewn valleys. It was the former that dominated after crossing the heritage railway line once more, climbing to briefly pass within touching distance of that morning's descent from Brenscombe Hill.

This trail carried me further west, along the upper slope of Nine Barrow Down at Ulwell, then I was clattering down Ballard Down to the sheer white stacks of Old Harry Rocks, which seemed to teeter uncertainly above the waves. On a laden bike and with tired legs I chose not to skirt too close to the edge, instead appreciating their magnitude from a respectful distance. From up here I could see Studland's sandy beach and couldn't avoid the temptation of dropping down to its southern tip to dip my aching feet in the sea, and came across an almost tropical scene: nestled by the beach under dappled shade sat a wooden shack, enticing sun bathers with the delicious aroma of Jamaican patties, of all things! It was too tempting a treat to pass up, so as the early evening air started to chill I found myself with a saltfish pattie and a mug of coffee in hand gazing across Studland Bay to the pure white cliffs of Old Harry Rocks, looking

uncannily like a gargantuan exclamation mark at the end of the mainland.

After a while I brushed the sand from my feet and pushed up to Ferry Road, which heads north to the chain link ferry that connects Studland to the millionaires' row of Sandbanks. However my destination did not lie across the bay, so half way along I headed inland along wide forest trails, the smell of pine returning to my nostrils, and in a haze of wood smoke found old friends at our rendezvous, hammocks and blankets already arranged round a fire. As the smell of cooking sausages mingled with the other heady scents lingering around our camp, my friends shared memories of their own family holidays here and while I decided that one day I'll come back and camp on that glorious spot by Swyre Head, for now, I thought, this will do just fine.

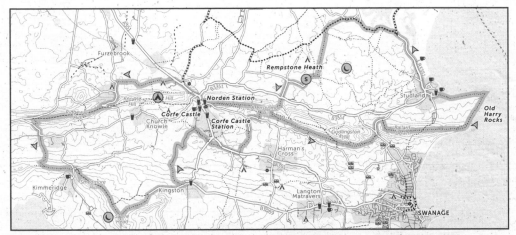

JURASSIC ROLLER COASTER

SIDMOUTH'S JURASSIC COASTLINE IS THE PERFECT PLACE TO EXPLORE SOUTH DEVON'S RICH RIDING POTENTIAL AND ANCIENT FOLKLORE ALIKE

Perhaps one of the most defining aspects of our small island is its coastline. Given that we are never further than 115km from the sea in Britain, it's easy to see why so many of us are drawn to it. Our island's 17,000-plus kilometres of coastline offers infinite variety, and bikepacking off-road gives you the opportunity to discover its richness and beauty in a way like no other.

Perhaps this is why, when looking to explore south Devon by bike, I almost subconsciously turned my wheels towards the Jurassic Coast and Sidmouth. I have ridden the Wessex Ridgeway before, which winds its way from Tollard Royal in Dorset to the handsome seaside town and World Heritage Site, Lyme Regis. But for a point-to-point ride it can be tricky, as both end points are far removed from rail connections.

I sketched out a loop that reached close to Honiton − once famous for its pottery and lace production, and now which now boasts London and Exeter rail connections − and swept down to the promenade in Sidmouth, its cycling heritage bolstered of late by the visit of the Tour of Britain, which has rolled out twice along its wide coastal road in recent years. Although the A-road that would take me from Honiton to the northernmost point of the ride can be fairly busy with midday traffic, it's just a half dozen kilometres, mostly labouring uphill, until I

INFO:

START/FINISH: Putts Corner, Gittisham EX10 0QQ, 50.759291, -3.211578

DISTANCE: 21.2 miles/34.2km   **ASCENT:** 2814ft/858m   **OFF-ROAD:** 70%

TERRAIN: Dirt bridleways, country lanes and tarmac cycle path along the Byes; climbs are few but tend to be steep.

NAVIGATION: Easy. With good signposting throughout, as well as some NCN Route 2 and 248 waymarks, this ride poses few navigational challenges. Just be careful not to turn off the main path through Mutter's Moor, and at the Bulverton Hill junction don't take the right turn down the slope but take the diagonal path due east that climbs initially. OS Landranger 192 covers this area.

EAT AND DRINK:

Clock Tower Café, Connaught Gardens, Peak Hill Road, Sidmouth, Devon EX10 8RZ, 01395 515319, www.clocktowercafesidmouth.co.uk

The Bowd Inn, Bowd, Sidmouth, Devon EX10 0ND, 01395 513328, www.thebowdinn.co.uk

SLEEP:

Blue Ball Inn, Steven's Cross, Sidford, EX10 9QL, 01395 514062, www.blueballinnsidford.co.uk

Camp: Coombe View Farm, Branscombe, Seaton, Devon EX12 3BT, 01297 680218, www.branscombe-camping.co.uk

Bivvy: near Conger Pool, Sandy Cove

PROVISIONS:

The Dairy Shop, 5 Church Street, Sidmouth, Devon EX10 8LY, 01395 513018

Cycle Service Shop and Café, The Old Post Office, Vicarage Road, Sidmouth, EX10 8TP 01395 513331, www.cycleservice.co.uk

would reach the exposed crossroads at Putts Corner and the beginnings of a coastal micro-adventure.

The Hare and Hounds, a large and lovely traditional pub in Sidbury, is steeped in folklore. In the 17th century it was a popular haunt for poachers and smugglers, while legend says the large stone outside dances at night when it hears the bells of Sidbury Church and rolls down the valley to drink at the River Sid. I was pleased to see it was looking suitably stationary as I rolled up on my bike. It was a little too early in the day to sample one of nearby Ottery St Mary's fine ales (I'm sure many a local has seen the stone move after one too many of these potent brews!), so I continued on, eager to explore this part of east Devon's Area of Outstanding Natural Beauty. It is easy to see why this glorious landscape has been given this designation, and riding through Farway Castle – not a castle at all but the site of a Bronze Age barrow cemetery – the grassy depressions were wispy with mist, and the rolling hills of conifers hushed and still. The dry, dusty bridleway guided me past an old airfield and up to the ridgeline of Harcombe Hill, from where I caught glimpses of the settlements to which the River Sid has imparted its name: thatched roofs giving the village of Sidbury a rattan-like texture from here; the busy junction at Sidford beyond that; the now gleaming whitewashed walls of Sidmouth further still.

Dropping down from Harcombe Hill, and still blessed with a continuous chain of bridleways, the sea glimmered beyond the canvas colony of Salcombe Regis' campsite. A short leg along the main road took me into quiet lanes that form part of the cycleway down to the coast. All signs of traffic disappeared as the lanes lead me into the Byes, a beautiful green corridor flanked by meadows and the treelined outskirts of the town that follows the course of the River Sid from Sidford to the sea. Only the final stretch from

the old Toll House took me back onto the road, splashing through the ford that surprisingly came up to my wheel hubs, before riding past a huge marquee erected for the town's renowned annual folk festival and down to the RNLI lifeboat launch.

As soon as I left the Byes behind I could smell the sea air and all my senses were stimulated as the promenade opened up before me. My ears rang with the noise of gulls, the rhythmic wax and wane of the waves over the pebbles, the throng of holidaymakers and locals alike. I headed down past the upturned rowing boats to a more secluded spot, favoured more by the odd dog-walker than hordes of day-trippers, kicked off my shoes and waded in, instantly vivified by the chill, choppy water. I looked back at my abandoned bike on the stony shore, remembering how only last year over in neighbouring Seaton violent storms had ripped the pebbles clean off the beach, leaving nothing but barren sandy stretches and battered beach huts – only to return the pebbles to their rightful place over the following weeks.

The sun was starting to hang heavy over Sidmouth's striking sandstone cliffs, so I dried off for a while on the shore before locking my bike up and exploring the town by foot. At the end of my sojourn, as the promenade began to empty and families retreated into their seafront hotels, I noticed a shallow-looking bay protected by a crescent of red cliff. On the top of one perched a café, closed at that hour, surrounded by formal gardens. With my morning coffee guaranteed I retrieved my bike and made my way across the pebbles, past what I later discovered to be a rocky outcrop called Chit Rocks, to my bed for the night on Tortoiseshell Rocks. I found a spot well back from the high tide mark, but far enough away from the soft sandstone cliff defaced by decades of gouged graffiti to give me a worry-free night's sleep – the eroding cliff face along the Jurassic Coast, all the way from

Orcombe Point near Exmouth to Old Harry's Rocks near Swanage in Dorset, has been responsible not only for bringing down roads and houses but also for the deaths of a number of people climbing, rock pooling or relaxing in their shadow.

Fashioning a makeshift windbreak from my tarp and bike frame I set up camp, making a small driftwood fire in a sheltered pebble basin, needing nothing more than a stove-cooked packet soup and a few nips of whisky from my hipflask to help me settle down for the night. I was far enough away from the town for its nocturnal activities not to disturb me, and let the soporific murmuring of the sea and a serene star-filled sky send me to sleep.

I was awake before dawn and sat contentedly staring out to sea, thinking how rarely we routine-ruled creatures get to see the sun rise, particularly over a scene such as the one that greeted me. As the first rays of sun glinted off the morning's mirror-calm sea, my desire for caffeine gradually over-rode that for daydreaming, and I gathered my things and made for the café on the cliff. It was a good choice for an early morning mocha, as it's on the NCN's route 2, which runs from Dover to St Austell, but for me would serve just as the southern-most tip of my ride.

Given that it runs up to Peak Hill I shouldn't have been surprised at the alarming gradient I had to cope with almost immediately. The reward for my exertions lay in the dappled sunlit corridors of Mutter's Moor and Bulverton Hill. I'm always sceptical when off-road routes pass through golf courses, but the fairways up here were among the most scenic I have ever encountered, snaking down through valley and vale toward the sea. In fact I began to miss their expansive vistas when I happened upon a dense, overgrown bridleway at Bulverton that was barely wider than my handlebars in places and left me nursing a collection of scratches and stings on every limb.

The old railway line through Harpford wood promised to be more spacious, however, and I was surprised to learn it is another NCN route (no.248), given how much it feels that nature is reclaiming the trail here. There's a deep, partially obscured gulley on one side and the surface is a mixture of mud and mulch, though of course, given its heritage, it is flat and uncomplicated. Before it reached the village of Tipton St John I peeled off and headed up a paved track which climbed steadily to the base of Beacon Hill, where a bridleway pointed me diagonally back over fields to a quiet country road leading into Ottery St Mary.

This small Devon town is the birthplace of the Romantic poet Samuel Taylor Coleridge, and is home to a unique flaming tar barrel procession which has become the centrepiece of the town's November carnival. It is believed the tradition stems from the lighting of barrels of pitch to warn of the invading Armada. I was a few months early for this incendiary experience, and unfortunately too late for Ottery's enchantingly titled Pixie Day in June, where children dress up and re-enact ancient folklore.

As I climbed out on bridleways and lanes up Westgate Hill towards Bellview Plantation, I could see the church of St Mary, a scaled-down version of Exeter Cathedral, standing squat in the heart of Ottery. I found myself pondering over the many tales I'd heard – of pirates and pixies, witches and smugglers – and wondered why this place is so alive with folk tradition. The 'Witches Stone', otherwise known as the 'Rolling Stone of Gittisham Common', loomed large before me as I wound up back at Putts Corner and the Hare and Hound. My only decision before heading back down Gittisham Hill to Honiton was whether to sample ales of the Otter or Branscombe breweries before I left. Better try both, I decided, leaning my bike against the Witches Stone.

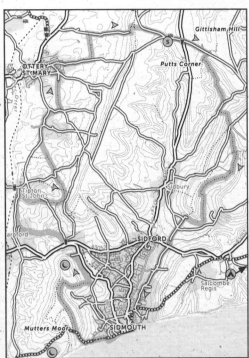

VALLEY OF THE ROCKS
– AN EXMOOR EPIC

A CHALLENGING FIGURE-OF-EIGHT RIDE ACROSS NORTH DEVON FROM RUGGED COAST TO VERDANT VALLEY

Where to begin exploring a national park that covers 700 square kilometres of moorland, wooded valleys and rocky coastline? Exmoor's sprawling terrain is incredibly varied, so it is difficult to get a real taste of the National Park in just one ride. Porlock and Dunkery Beacon would have been a great choice, but a friend and I decided to head further west to another place that promised wonderful views, incredible single-track and still encapsulates what it is to ride and camp in Exmoor. We headed out towards Simonsbath, on the furthest fringe of west Somerset, in his stripped-out VW T4, hoping against hope that we didn't have to use its interior to sleep in. Given the forecast, as I've learned previously, it's always wise to have a plan B.

We were headed to the worryingly named Breakneck Hole, to ride in a figure-of-eight north across the moors, dropping down the cliffs from Lynton into Lynmouth and back along the Two Moors Way into Simonsbath, where the banks of the River Barle would provide a wild camp site for the night. As we arrived in Simonsbath, evidence of the moor's constant and often severe undulations was all around

---

INFO:

START/FINISH: Car Park, Simonsbath TA24 7SH, 51.140150, -3.753494

DISTANCE: 46.6 miles/75.0km   **ASCENT:** 6945ft/2117m   **OFF-ROAD:** 85%

TERRAIN: Peaty moorland, stony singletrack and river paths. Plenty of climbs and occasional river crossings.

NAVIGATION: Difficult. The bridleways across the moorland, particularly on the northern half of the ride, can be faint or almost non-existent at times. Although the Two Moors Way is signposted on the way south from Cheriton it is easy to drop down into Farley Water by mistake, so make sure you keep right at Roborough Castle. Stay right further along Cheriton Ridge too, to avoid crossing Clannon Ball (steep and very rocky) and meeting the road too soon. OS Landranger 180 would be useful.

EAT AND DRINK:

The Rockford Inn, Brendon, North Devon EX35 6PT, 01598 741214, www.therockfordinn.co.uk
The Village Inn, 19 Lynmouth Street, Lynton, Devon EX35 6EH, 01598 752354, www.thevillageinnexmoor.co.uk

SLEEP:

Exmoor Forest Inn, Simonsbath, Minehead, TA24 7SH, 01643 831341, www.exmoorforestinn.co.uk
Camp: Caffyns Farm, Croscombe Lane, Lynton EX35 6JW, 01598 753967, www.exmoorcoastholidays.co.uk
Bivvy: woods by Cow Castle, River Barle

PROVISIONS:

Boeveys Tea Rooms, Simonsbath, Minehead TA24 7SH, 01643 831622
Exmoor Bike, Unit 1 Enterprise Centre, Enterprise Park, Minehead, Somerset TA24 5AE, 07920 047901, www.exmoorbike.com

us. Wave upon wave of steep-sided valleys seemed to ripple across the moors. Given that our main port of call that day across the peaty moor tops would be Lynton, whose well-earned epithets include 'Valley of the Rocks' and 'Little Switzerland', we understood this off-road adventure had all the makings of an epic journey. Yet, despite its name, Breakneck Hole was kind to us, rolling out heavy but relatively flat peat tracks ahead of us. We'd gained the high ground travelling to Simonsbath, yet we would lose all 450 metres of it on our descent into Lynmouth; the rest of the day would be all about reclaiming it.

Our ride across the moor tops was windswept, though peaceful nonetheless. Sheep grazed among the gorse bushes and heather, but there was no sign of the ponies that are so emblematic of Exmoor. I hoped to catch a glimpse of one of the hundreds of red deer that live scattered across this former royal hunting forest, but they too were conspicuous only by their absence. Our laboured excursions across the moor were soon allayed by a gradual hard-packed track that became metalled as it dropped to a valley at Cherrybridge. Between holiday chalets and farmsteads we descended further, through wooded singletrack before opening onto dramatic, splintered coastal cliffs. The fantastically Gothic Lee Abbey sits here, at the western mouth to the Valley of the Rocks. Some 230 years ago the original mansion here, and nine acres of its estate, succumbed to a landslide and fell away into the sea. Lee Abbey sits a little safer inland now, its grounds a gated religious retreat. Instead of taking the road down into Lynmouth Bay we chose to walk the dicey path along the cliff face – a much better way to experience this rugged coastline in all its glory. Another would be the funicular cliff railway, a Victorian water-powered lift connecting the twin towns, but we'd have struggled to get ourselves and two loaded bikes into its compact compartments.

Described by the artist Thomas Gainsborough as "the most delightful place for a landscape painter this country can boast", Lynmouth, and its harbour in particular, is indeed picturesque, though probably quite different from Gainsborough's time. A severe flood in 1952 wrecked more than a hundred buildings here; the river is now diverted to flow round the town.

A road bridge past inviting-looking pubs looking out to sea took us over the East Lyn River and to the foot of a climb on which even motorised traffic seemed to struggle. There was no funicular to take us up this one-in-four incline, but at least a grassy bridleway offered to take us off the tarmac and, at last, back out onto the moors. Once more we were rising and falling with the landscape; plunging down valleys to cross the river by bridge, then rising briefly much like a swimmer taking a quick gulp of air, before diving down to the water once more – at Watersmeet we had no option but to ford the river at knee level.

Our journey back onto the moors was an altogether different affair. Whereas our passage north was across heavy moors capped in yellow and purple heather, our journey back to Simonsbath was at first on wide, stony bridleway, then rock-strewn descents to follow the path of Hoar Oak Water along the valley floor, before at last returning to familiar barren, grassy expanses. We were followed, quite unnervingly, by cattle for some distance; the herd keeping pace behind our wheels. Eventually we shook them off in a fog that seemed to drift in from nowhere, and then the squall we had hoped wouldn't come hit us full in the face. It was all the impetus our tired legs needed to get off the moors and seek shelter in Simonsbath's rambling old pub. Its glowing hearth was a welcome sight and we kicked off sodden shoes while supping Exmoor ales.

We bought some time by sitting out the rain over dinner. I'd have much preferred to be cooking

here by the devil for a bet, and we decided to have our own wager as we freewheeled down towards it.

Trying to clear all 55 metres of the wet and uneven stone slabs, which are a metre wide at best, without putting a foot down was tricky enough; to do so amid a crowd of onlookers, facing oncoming pedestrians and with the threat of a very wet landing should you lose your balance should be rewarded with more than just a pint of beer, but that was the stake as my companion struck out first. Whereas he cleared the bridge unfalteringly, I failed – a foot down meant that I would be buying – but at least I escaped with my dignity intact. As 4x4s forded the river next to us, we left Tarr Steps behind, inching up a beast of a rocky bridle path that took us slowly off the valley floor. Our passage back towards Simons-bath traversed lush green meadows for a while, before we disappeared into the trees to find our final fording point. When we did, it was the deepest yet – at the half-way point we were nearly waist deep, and the current threatened to tear our bikes from our grasp. But our dry-bags acted as impromptu buoyancy aids and we struggled across loose, slippery stones to find a firmer bed at the river's edge. Our final leg took us back onto the moors for a while, but the ride's watery theme continued. With shoes and shorts sodden, and all lubrication washed from our creaking bikes, we crossed the river one final time – by bridge thankfully – to return to our camp at Cow Castle before retracing our tracks along the river's edge, and that sumptuous single-track, to Simonsbath.

my own down by the river, but we'd have been doing ourselves no favours putting tarps up in the pouring rain. Yet just as we were about to give up hope and retire to the van, the weather broke, and in the twilight we took the opportunity to ride back out, south this time along the Barle, to camp among the trees near a hillock called Cow Castle. Rigging the tarp under a tight pine canopy gave us a good chance of staying dry, and luckily it was the murmur of the Barle rather than the drumming of rain that we fell asleep to.

Packing up early the next morning under patchy skies, we set off through the valley in a bid to make headway in the dry. The path here was wonderfully technical – it echoed the meanders of the river for a time, and roots and rocks made for a tactile treat after the heavy peat of the day before. Then the Two Moors Way lived up to its name and sent us out onto its rolling expanse once more, before tarmac took us down to the village of Withypool. By a miniscule automotive museum we found a lovely little café, where we hurriedly refuelled under darkening skies. Two more river fordings sandwiched our crossing of Tarr Steps, a stone clapper bridge possibly dating back to 1000 BC. Local legend has it that the stones, which weigh more than a ton apiece, were placed

I was happy to settle our wager at the bar before climbing into dry clothes in the back of the van. I was also glad this was all we'd used its bare interior for, and that we'd persevered with our wild camp last night. Camping out on a ride gives you a much better feel for a place, and I felt I knew Exmoor a little better, having spent a night in its embrace.

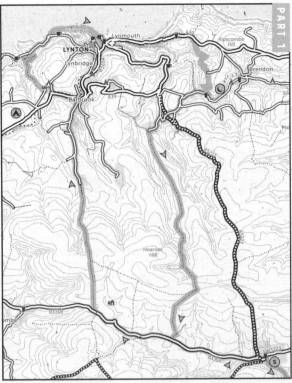

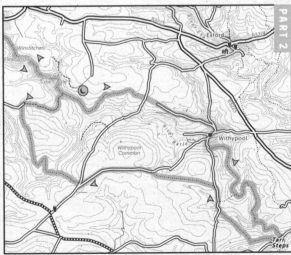

A TASTE OF THE TORS

A TRULY TESTING ROUTE IN DARTMOOR'S NORTH-EAST CORNER WILL GIVE EVEN EXPERIENCED ADVENTURE RIDERS A RUN FOR THEIR MONEY

There is a time for riding and wild camping on the exposed plains of Dartmoor, and the short days and temperamental conditions of late autumn are probably not it. Yet the very nature of exploring and discovering the British wilderness, I have found, involves immersing yourself in the terrain, exposing yourself to the elements and experiencing the land around you with each and every sense, even if that involves the feeling of lashing rain on your face or muddy water seeping through your shoes...

A friend and I came ready for the rain, donning numerous layers capped with waterproof shells, but it was a ferocious wind that caused us the most immediate problems, whipping our hoods and snapping at cuffs. My friend's compact little camper van had never looked so inviting as we left it parked and ventured out onto Headland Warren on our bikes. We made certain of our position before heading too far, so faint were the trails and so vast the moorland before us. We were on the north-east fringe of Dartmoor, and civilization, in the form of Tavistock and Okehampton, lay far to the west over huge swathes of remote moor used solely for military exercises.

INFO:

START/FINISH: Bennett's Cross car park, Chagford Common PL20 6TA, 50.619883, -3.866134

DISTANCE: 34.7 miles/55.8km   **ASCENT:** 5547ft/1691m   **OFF-ROAD:** 75%

TERRAIN: Peaty moorland tracks, riverside forest trails and country lanes. The ride starts at its highest point, so three of the four significant climbs are left until near the end.

NAVIGATION: Challenging, particularly on the southwestern part of the ride. The bridleway from the car park on Bush Down is not signposted; neither are the network of paths around Grimspound. On the outward journey stay left around Shapley Tor, and returning via Grimspound keep right on Hameldown Tor. A compass and OS Landranger 191 are recommended for this ride.

EAT AND DRINK:

Bridford Inn, Bridford, Exeter, Devon EX6 7HT, 01647 252250, www.bridfordinn.co.uk

The Cleave, Lustleigh, Devon TQ13 9TJ, 01647 277223, www.thecleavelustleigh.uk.com

SLEEP:

Royal Oak Inn, Dunsford, Exeter, Devon EX6 7DA, 01647 252256, www.royaloakd.com

Sweet Meadows & Wild Woods camping, Clifford Bridge, Drewsteignton, Devon EX6 6QB, 01647 24331

Bivvy: edge of Bridford Woods

PROVISIONS:

Michael Howard Butcher & Delicatessen, 7 Court Street, Moretonhampstead, Devon TQ13 8NE, 01647 440267, www.michael-howard-butchers.co.uk

The Bike Fixer, Unit A4, Cranafords Industrial Park, Chagford, Devon TQ13 8DR, 07717 046064, www.chagfordbikefixer.com

Our path was to the east, though, to the village of Dunsford on the National Park's perimeter, and the ride from a car park on the lonely road high up on the moor between Princetown and Moretonhampstead would be predominantly downhill. Our journey towards the River Bovey was by no means easy going though. Not only did the wind toss stinging raindrops relentlessly against our cheeks, but the saturated ground sucked at our wheels and feet, making progress ponderous at best. The thistle- and scrub-capped earth was shallow on the moors, the granite rocks that rose their heads along the boggy trail never far from the surface, so it didn't take much rain to turn large tracts of moor to quagmire. I was glad though to have given up with clipless pedals and cleats after my summer rides; flat pedals made the constant dabbing of feet or dismounting to push that much easier, and both needed to be done regularly here. The stone outcrops on every tor gave occasional shelter, though, and we found ourselves scurrying from one cairn to another to hunker down and check our position before heading back out into the headwind.

At last, from nearly 500 metres up on Shapley Tor, the respite of a valley beckoned. A wide, grassy doubletrack soon ushered us down the upper slopes before twin stone ribbons either side of a churned-up gulley whisked us down a steep embankment, away from the torrid moor tops to the sheltered wooded valley of North Bovey. The peat mires (known as 'feather beds' or 'quakers' by locals) were now behind us; the following day though, we would be climbing to make their acquaintance once more. Though down off the tors, the gradient turned against us; along the lanes around North Bovey and Moretonhampstead we seemed to be running perpendicular to a series of lower ridges and were constantly climbing to meet them. Finally, close to Dartmoor's boundary, we inched our way to the last cairn we would see, up on Mardon Down, below which the woods that embrace the banks of the River Teign would give us refuge for the night.

Our ride was not done for the day though. A forgotten country lane dropped us down into Cod Wood, its crumbling tarmac buried under layers of mud and leaves. We crossed the Teign at Clifford Barton's ancient bridge before tackling a delightful section of technical wooded singletrack that followed the river for over 2 kilometres. The village of Dunsford, nestled nearby on the National Park boundary, marked the furthest point on our loop. The wooded banks of the Teign offered plenty of scope for camping – neither of us fancied an exposed camp on the moors – so we headed into the village in search of warmth and hospitality having not seen a soul all afternoon. The convivial bar of Dunsford's village pub made up for our so-far solitary sojourn; it was clearly the hub of this attractive little Devon village, and we were made to feel welcome by locals keen to understand why anyone would ride across the moors in these conditions.

It was through talking to them that I began to understand the inherent dangers of remote moorland riding, particularly if unprepared or naive. My compass was crucial in getting us off the tops at times, with my GPS failing to find a signal. So many unmapped paths criss-cross the moors, any of which can tempt you off your route and disorient you. The bogs can be dangerously deep and even the shallow ones can exhaust you. And that's when the elements begin to grind you down, we were told. Noticing the darkening skies looking calmer, we returned to the woods on the Teign's south bank, finding a plateau a way off the path up the steep wooded bank and before long tent, tarp and hammock were set up round a smouldering cook fire. We were surprised by how late we managed to sit out by the flames before fatigue and the chill air drove us under tarpaulin at last.

After being woken by showers, early morning brought a sight to stir the soul. With a fullish moon still hanging lazily beyond Dunsford, a rainbow framed the village church immaculately – a complete crescent of bright, oily hues dissected perfectly by the narrow spire. We packed up still marvelling at this backdrop as the sun's rays crept further across the nearby pastures; previously looking so dank and sodden, this morning a heartening patchwork of russets and golds. Our departure was also a contrast to yesterday's, as we loaded up the bikes with an eagerness noticeably absent before.

The world about us was silent as we saddled up and headed for hushed byways blanketed with matted leaves. We rolled through Bridford's still sleeping streets and made our way toward the forested trails of Laployd Plantation. Alongside its reservoirs we enjoyed flowing forest trails, barrelling with abandon down root-riddled tracks. It was the last time our path would stay horizontal, and we were making the most of it. From here there was a fantastic rock garden through the woods of Lustleigh Cleave, along a trail marked 'Nut Crackers', a detour from our planned route but such fun to ride we barely noticed we were climbing.

This blissful ignorance didn't last though – we were heading for Greathound Tor, up a greasy slope that was hellishly steep, where feet proved to have little more traction than tyres. The gradient eased off towards Grimspound, and atop one of the highest tors for miles around we were able to see what we were blind to yesterday – Dartmoor in all its wild, untameable beauty. The Two Moors Way ran across our path here, continuing north to Devon's rugged north coast at Lynmouth, and south to Ivybridge on Dartmoor's southern fringe. The long-distance path was quite pronounced, despite us returning to the seemingly impenetrable peat bogs close to Headland Warren. Our trail, however, was less discernible, and cut deep into old mine workings nestled between the tors. More than once we lost all trace of it, either doubling back or cutting across thick scrub to rejoin the trail where it re-emerged. Every time called for careful consultation of map and compass.

We were almost there, but a wrong turn even then could have sent us blindly off-course. Even in clearer weather there were so few distinguishable features to use as points of reference, just a complex jigsaw of moor, tor, thistle and granite. Once or twice the disarming sight of a partial animal carcass reminded us we really had returned to the wild after our comfortable night on the outskirts of civilization. As the weather inevitably closed in once more, hastening our push off the moors, we made out a thin strip in the distance, the only linear object in a world of gradual natural transition. It was the Princetown road, and alongside it the camper van we had left a little over a day ago. We could have returned to the relative warmth of the van last night but I'd have missed that feeling of immersing myself in an unknown place. After all, you only really discover a place by getting lost in it – sometimes literally as well as metaphorically, I find – and Dartmoor is a wild and wonderful place I could really lose myself in. I have just discovered a small corner of it.

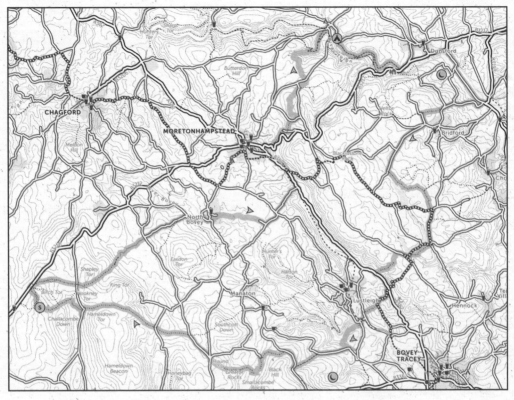

THE
SOUTH
EAST

A GREEN RIBBON THROUGH THE BIG SMOKE

A WONDERFUL DAY'S OFF-ROAD RIDING CAN BE FOUND IN SOUTH LONDON, LINKING PARKS AND COMMONS WITH THE THAMES PATH AND LEAVING THE TRAFFIC BEHIND

When I moved to London in my late teens I hadn't yet been bitten by the mountain biking bug. Even when I had discovered the joy of cross-country riding, I figured even the suburban parts of the capital were too built-up and congested to take advantage of the freedom an off-road bike promised. So I'd go further afield, to the North Downs or Surrey Hills and on away days to Brighton or Sheffield to tackle the South Downs or Peaks. Yet unbeknownst to me then, South London offers a snaking chain of royal parks and open common land unrivalled by any area in the city and its outlying districts, perhaps with the exception of Epping Forest.

Having moved away some time ago, I devised an almost exclusively off-road 30km route from Kew Gardens to Hampton, taking in the royal land of Richmond and Bushy Parks, together with

INFO:

START: Kew Gardens station, Station Approach TW9 3BZ, 51.477158, -0.284806
FINISH: Hampton station, Ashley Road TW12 2HU, 51.416019, -0.371843

DISTANCE: 19.5 miles/31.5km   **ASCENT:** 1079ft/329m   **OFF-ROAD:** 85%

TERRAIN: Wide gravel doubletrack, open parkland, woodland paths, muddy bridleways and occasional minor roads. Flat and easy going, with occasional climbs in Richmond Park.

NAVIGATION: Easy. The Thames Path and NCN Route 4 are waymarked, and signing through the parks and commons is excellent. There are a number of paths through each green space, particularly Richmond Park; if in doubt keep in sight of the park roads. You'll need to check www.royalparks.org.uk for opening times for Bushy Park and Richmond Park. OS Landranger 176 will help you negotiate the transitions between parks.

EAT AND DRINK:

Boho Café, 159a King's Road, Kingston upon Thames KT2 5JF, www.bohocafe.co.uk

Boaters Inn, Canbury Gardens, Lower Ham Road, Kingston-Upon-Thames KT2 5AU, 020 8541 4672, www.boaterskingston.com

SLEEP:

Fox & Grapes, 9 Camp Road, London SW19 4UN, 020 8619 1300, www.foxandgrapeswimbledon.co.uk

Bivvy: Caesar's Camp, Wimbledon Common

PROVISIONS:

Oliver's Wholefood Store, Kew Gardens station, 020 8948 3990

Active Cycles, 219 Lower Mortlake Road Richmond TW9 2LN, 020 8940 3717, www.active-cycles.co.uk

Old Deer Park, Putney Heath and Wimbledon Common, using the Thames Path and very occasional road sections to link them. Even in the Big Smoke, I'd realised, you could trail ride for a day through wide-open green spaces, and wild camp, with the feeling of being somewhere altogether more remote than the nation's capital city.

I disembarked at Kew Gardens station. The little triangle of independent shops, delis and cafés give it a real village-like feel, and the lovely platform pub The Tap On The Line, with such large windows it feels like an orangerie, was the perfect place for a pre-ride coffee (or post-ride beer if you were to do this ride the other way around). However the skies were looking leaden, so I rolled around the walls of Kew Gardens, past the imposing main gates and ducked down what is little more than an alley – Ferry Lane – to the Thames Path. Looking out across the river to the barges along Brentford Ait, I revelled in the relative seclusion on this side of the river. It was quite overgrown here, with stagnant, marshy water half-hidden by almost tropical-looking vines and trees on one side, and the grey, murky Thames on the other; at points the path was little more than a stony tunnel through the trees.

Kew Gardens and Old Deer Park offer no real access to bikes (almost two-thirds of the latter's 150 hectares are classed as private) but from the Thames Path their green expanse is still easily appreciated. As I rode on, the east bank opened out into Syon Park, landscaped in the 18th century by Capability Brown, and for a brief moment I was encompassed by green space on all sides – from the flood meadows on the opposite bank to the golf course on Old Deer Park, and even Isleworth Ait stretching out in the middle of the river ahead. Within a kilometre or so, though, St Margarets gave the opposite bank an altogether more urban profile, and as I passed Richmond lock and headed

under the Twickenham Road bridge, Richmond opened up in front of me – the riverside pubs and bars, the boat-building workshops beneath the arches, and launches and pleasure cruisers lined up end-to-end between the bridges.

I continued under Richmond Bridge and soon left the riverside behind, dropping down the gears to cope with a sharp climb up Nightingale Lane, past what I expected to be the Royal Star and Garter Home, built for injured servicemen after the First World War. It has now become a £50 million luxury apartment development. Some things were bound to have changed in the 15 years I'd been away.

The brief clamour of traffic died away as I rode into Richmond Park. Bound by speed restrictions, the cars moved procession-like along the road, and while the dedicated cycle path around the perimeter was equally busy, I took to the gravelled horse tracks in between, then rode 'off-piste' across the park. The high brick walls around the perimeter help seal you off from the urban sprawl here, and only the outline of some Roehampton high-rise apartments and the faintest shimmer of the City of London miles beyond give the game away in this peaceful patch of London.

Crows cawed from fallen, hollow tree stumps as I passed Sheen Cross Wood, re-joining a sandy stretch of bridleway, before the London traffic once again assaulted my senses at Roehampton Gate. That was all the encouragement I needed to pick up the pace past towering university halls of residence, and once across the A-road, I was within striking distance of tranquil space once more, this time on Putney Heath. I avoided the tempting Youngs pubs en route, and struck out across the heath. A statuesque heron among the reeds of Scio Pond stopped me briefly in my tracks; I paused to marvel at the presence of such a majestic creature, before a subway whisked

me away, out onto chewed-up muddy horse tracks, along which the heath faded away and the common unfurled before me.

I rounded the once-familiar windmill, a 200-year-old, Grade II listed building which is something of a landmark in south-west London, though I noticed its sails had disappeared since I was last here. The feeling of space was glorious, the only interruption to my ride across the common being my cautious glances up and down the golf club's fairways, before traversing their rights of way. My destination was the Fox and Grapes pub up near Caesar's Camp, the remains of an Iron Age hillfort thought to have been occupied some 500 years before the Roman emperor was born. I couldn't resist a pint of their locally brewed craft lager before carrying on with my route. My camp for the night was a stone's throw from Caesar's own, at the common's highest point before the track drops down through the woods to Putney Vale and my first port of call the following morning, Robin Hood Gate, which would take me back into Richmond Park's tranquil plains.

I must have slept well because as I rose from my slumber the sounds of the common users – the horse riders, the joggers and the privileged few who live in this exclusive spot – were discernible in the distance. I hurtled down the stony track of Robin Hood Lane, past the Richardson Evans training ground, and pedalled languidly back into Richmond Park, intending to take its southern fringe this time to Kingston Gate and back down to the river.

Rain the night before had made the sandy horse trails heavy going so I stuck to firmer, though fainter, undesignated tracks, through the dense copse of Isabella Plantation before finding a surprisingly steep climb near the perimeter wall

that fired up my sleepy synapses. I left Kingston Gate and took a succession of back streets down to the Thames at Canbury Gardens. The path past the boathouse was paved, and busy at this hour, but there was plenty of room for manoeuvre, before my road transitioned over Kingston Bridge and into Hampton Wick. There's a station here, but to end the ride now would have meant missing out on one last foray through prized London green space. High walls keep Bushy Park, London's second largest royal park at 445 hectares, secreted away and, unlike Richmond, it is dissected by just a single road leading to the Diana memorial fountain and allowing access to the park's café. Although the tarmac path of Cobbler's Walk is also a permissive bridleway, the best riding is to be had off the beaten track. Often many of the 300-strong deer that inhabit the park – they seemed much less timid than those in Richmond – wander unfazed onto the path and take up residence there, so you'll end up on the grass anyway.

The turning weather made it difficult for me to fully appreciate this space; I'd have liked to have spent time exploring the numerous plantations, buildings and ponds scattered around the park. Instead I sought shelter in the Waterhouse Woodland Garden, a small, enclosed nature reserve, before pushing the bike the last few hundred metres to Hampton's open air pool (not only because I had punctured; there's no cycling beyond the woodland garden) and the main road. From here, Hampton station is barely a kilometre away.

As I awaited the warmth of a railway carriage there, I couldn't help but wonder how many frustrated London cyclists know you can ride for an entire day in the capital, and for only a tiny fraction of that time share your journey with any cars. I do now, and I miss London all the more for it.

	MILES	YARDS
RICHMOND GATE	1	1140
ROEHAMPTON GATE	—	1450
ROBIN HOOD GATE	2	190
BY ROEHAMPTON		
" " "	1	1490
BY WHITE LODGE		
KINGSTON GATE	3	200
HAM GATE	2	760

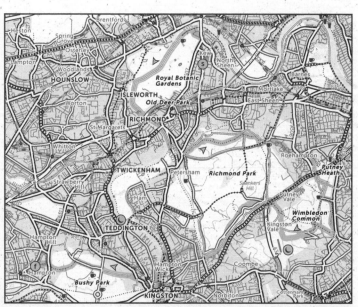

LONDON'S GREENEST GATEWAY

ANCIENT EPPING FOREST, A ROYAL HUNTING SITE, PROMISES A LEAFY ESCAPE FROM THE CONFINES OF THE CAPITAL

I quietly envy those who reside in the London Borough of Hackney. Not only can they enjoy the area's rich cultural diversity, its hipster hangouts and the legacy of the Olympic Games in the form of the Queen Elizabeth Olympic Park, but there is also a spider's web of cycle trails and a significant swathe of green space in which to escape the chaos of the capital. With lovely stretches of open land such as Victoria Park or Hackney Marshes, Hackney also holds the key to Epping Forest, a strip of forest trails running from Forest Gate to Epping that would make a perfect night's escape for north London or Essex-based mountain bikers seeking a wild camping fix.

Just north of Stratford, around Whipps Cross, Epping Forest gradually begins to open out as it winds its way north through the south-west corner of Essex. Once the hunting ground of English kings, its ancient woodlands, lakes, heaths and glades offer a peaceful retreat from the heaving metropolis and sprawling urbanity of this most populated corner of the south-east, and it was the forest's most southerly point I headed to in search of a rare taste of 'wild' London.

A friend joined me on my journey, keen to experience one more wild weekend away before the birth of his first child. I couldn't promise him a

INFO:

START: Forest Gate station, Woodgrange Road E7 0NF, 51.549146, 0.022075
FINISH: Cheshunt station, Station Approach EN8 9AQ, 51.701564, -0.020342

DISTANCE: 19.1miles/30.8km   **ASCENT:** 1243ft/379m   **OFF-ROAD:** 90%

TERRAIN: Undesignated forest tracks – most are soft earth, often muddy, occasionally technical, with rooty sections and grassy bridle paths. Flat or very gentle gradients.

NAVIGATION: Easy. OS Explorer 174 could be a useful companion, but Epping Forest's trails are well signposted and NCN Route 1 will guide you towards Cheshunt station.

EAT AND DRINK:

The Horseshoes, Horseshoe Hill, Upshire, Essex, EN9 3SN, 01992 712745, www.thehorseshoes-countrypub.co.uk
The Larder, Butler's Retreat, 12 Ranger's Road, London E4 7QH, 020 7998 7858, www.worldslarder.co.uk

SLEEP:

Duke of Wellington, Wellington Hill, High Beech IG10 4AH, 020 8502 1620, www.dukeofwellingtonhighbeech.co.uk
Lee Valley Campsite, Sewardstone Road, Waltham Abbey, Chingford, Essex E4 7RA, 020 8529 5689, www.visitleevalley.org.uk
Bivvy: Bury Wood

PROVISIONS:

Coffee 7, 10 Sebert Road, Forest Gate, London E7 0NQ, 020 8534 7774, www.coffee7.co.uk
Go Further Cycling, Forest Lodge Commercial Complex, Epping Road, Epping, Essex CM16 5HW, 01992 815132, www.gofurthercycling.co.uk

true wilderness on this occasion, but the experience of camping out so close to the capital is one all of its own.

At last on our way, we resolved to reach Forest Gate with a little more urgency, although at only 19km in length, Epping Forest can be covered in a couple of hours, and would be perfect for a mini adventure with kids. We were in no rush, however, and I had extended our route to the north-west to incorporate some of the open green space found in the Lee Valley Regional Park (taking in the park's entire length, from Waltham Cross to Ware would double the length of the ride). Soon we had left Leyton behind and were riding along Lake House Road, past the ponds on Wanstead Flat, still deep in the heart of East London. A cycle path took us off our last road for nearly 25 kilometres, and ahead lay the promise of Bush Wood and the shade of Epping Forest on what was a surprisingly warm early autumn afternoon.

There was a cacophony of traffic noise overhead as an underpass took us beneath the Whipps Cross Road, but the ancient trees that rise up around Hollow Pond, a popular boating lake, soon muffled it, and before long we were riding through boggy forest paths soft with rotting leaves, exposed only to dappled sunlight and the voices of boaters on the pond. There are occasional roads that dissect the forest across its axis, but they are few and far between, and on our journey, at least, free from traffic. Epping Forest is just 4km at its widest, and covers an area just shy of 2,500 hectares, but its shape, form and vegetation vary continuously. One moment we were ducking under low-slung boughs and branches of oaks, birches, holly or beech trees; the next we were out on ancient pasture following a whisper of single-track or riding from glade to shade and back again while skirting ponds, crossing wooded bridges and traversing dried-up stream beds.

In this Site of Special Scientific Interest, many of the trees have taken on a peculiar appearance. These 'pollarded' trees haven't been cut since the Epping Forest Act was passed in 1878 and have since grown massive crowns of thick trunk-like branches and strangely bulbous bores; their branches can often no longer be supported by the parent tree, so the large amount of dead wood in the forest supports numerous rare species of invertebrates and fungi.

Before we approached another underpass at the North Circular we caught fleeting glimpses of late Victorian semis through the trees, then a school, and soon a clearing lined with terraced cottages that looked for all the world like some bucolic English village green. Our proximity to this arterial highway soon dispelled that illusion, but as ever on our route through the forest our dalliance with tarmac was a brief and detached one, and within moments we were pushing up a steep bank and were back into the woods once more. The further north we went the more open the forest began to feel, and we crossed whole swathes of heathland and pasture that is still used by cattle – so warning signs by the road informed us – though there was no sign of any livestock.

Mid-war houses began to encroach on our passage once more around Highams Park boating lake, before a harsh metallic crack alerted us to a fairway through the trees belonging to Woodford Golf Club. But then our route was once again reclaimed by rolling heathland – over Hatch Plain and Whitehall Plain – and hedgerows laden with autumn berries, while the River Ching flowed gently alongside the trail. It was at the old Ranger's Road, that runs down into Chingford, that we came across a splendid Tudor mansion and two less ornate but equally handsome buildings, the Queen Elizabeth Hunting Lodge and Butler's Retreat. The Lodge,

originally called the Great Standing, was commissioned by Henry VIII in 1543 as a place from which to view the chase at Chingford, and later renovated for Queen Elizabeth I. Butler's Retreat, where we stopped for a coffee and filled our bottles from its fountain, is one of the few remaining retreats in the forest, and still adheres to its Temperance principles of serving non-alcoholic refreshments, having been converted into a café in 2012.

As Butler's Retreat closed to its visitors, who had flocked to take in the views over Connaught Water, Woodman's Glade and beyond, we struck out in search of a camping location, which we found in a clearing in Bury Wood. We were deep enough into the forest for our presence to go unannounced, and we found a spot where four birches offered a fine place to sling our hammocks. Because of local bylaws forbidding the lighting of fires in the forest, we had to make do with a piping hot brew and a tot of whisky to keep the evening chill at bay. As the heat of the day quickly receded, we talked beneath the stars – in a glade in a small Essex forest – about how unlikely a spot this had seemed for an adventure ride, yet how memorable it had already become.

Removing all traces of our stay the next morning we headed out through the faded grassy plains toward High Beach, never too far from Epping New Road, the only real stretch of road to split the forest north-south now that the plain spills over it and rolls down into Loughton. It is here that Lopping Hall was built after the Epping Forest Act as compensation to commoners denied their 'lopping' rights in a bid to protect the forest.

I hadn't really considered that the forest lay on a ridge (between the valleys of the rivers Lea and Roding) but since our stop at Butler's Retreat the views across the now-thinning forest and down the slopes from the ridge line had become more and more impressive. The only blot on the landscape is the M25, where the forest seems to be repelled by this vast tract of tarmac, and although it doesn't disappear entirely before reaching Epping on the other side, we opted to continue our green belt ride, peeling off from the forest path onto a bridleway heading north-east below the motorway. The Forest Way ensured our progress beyond the M25 was mostly hard-packed bridle path, before we briefly felt roads again for the first time in a day's riding. Then our route took us deep into the heart of the Lee Valley Regional Park, meandering down between the River Lea and Hooks Marsh, then alongside Cheshunt Lake before the town, its station, and home beckoned. It had been a joy, riding in such tranquillity, when all around the world continued apace, with us blissfully unaware of any of it. It may have been called 'the people's forest' by Queen Victoria, but for the past 24 hours Epping Forest had felt like ours alone.

FINDING EFRAFA

THE ANCIENT WAYFARERS WALK CUTS A PICTURESQUE PATH FROM THE VALE OF PEWSEY ALL THE WAY TO THE REAL WARRENS OF WATERSHIP DOWN

Some of my journeys around Britain have been inspired by literary connections with the area, but none more overtly than this route through the North Wessex Downs Area of Outstanding Natural Beauty. I was torn between a Ridgeway ride out of Marlborough to the north-west or a meander through the Chilterns up to the north-east, but chose this ride for the book partly because of its rail connections at either end, partly because of the beautiful simplicity of the trail, but primarily because it climbs up onto the famous Watership Down.

You might be surprised to learn that the downland inhabited by the likes of Bigwig, General Woundwort and Hazel is not a fictional place at all, and not only did author Richard Adams draw inspiration from these picturesque downs and wealds, but he has spent much of his life in these parts, from Newbury in Berkshire as a schoolboy to Whitchurch in Hampshire, where he still resides, so he knew the warrens on the downs intimately.

My journey followed a similar path, beginning on the Wiltshire/Berkshire border, at a diminutive

---

INFO:

START: Bedwyn station, The Knapp SN8 5RD, 51.380035, -1.598998
FINISH: Overton tation, Station Hill RG25 3JG, 51.253480, -1.258779

DISTANCE: 24.0 miles/38.6km   **ASCENT:** 2162ft/659m   **OFF-ROAD:** 85%

TERRAIN: Stone, chalk, grass and dirt bridleways and byways, and occasional country lanes. After a sharp climb to the downs the trail is smooth and undulating.

NAVIGATION: Easy. The Wayfarer's Walk and other local routes are waymarked along most of this ride and it is all bridleway and byway. The only problem can be finding the diagonal path up Inkpen Hill and its continuation through crop fields at the top of the hill. The gated bridleway up the slope is hidden beneath an overhanging tree. Once up the slope keep the fence-line on your left. Use OS Landranger 174.

EAT AND DRINK:

The Harrow at Little Bedwyn, Marlborough, Wiltshire SN8 3JP, 01672 870871, www.theharrowatlittlebedwyn.com
Indigo Palace at The Crown & Anchor, Ham, Wiltshire SN8 3RB, 01488 668896, www.indigopalace.co.uk

SLEEP:

The Crown & Garter, Great Common Rd, Inkpen Common, RG17 9QR, 01488 668325
Postern Hill Campsite, Salisbury Hill, Marlborough, Wiltshire SN8 4ND, 01672 515195, www.campingintheforest.co.uk
Bivvy: Watership Down

PROVISIONS:

Great Bedwyn Post Office, 90 Church St, Great Bedwyn SN8 3PF, 01672 870673, www.greatbedwynpost.co.uk
Banjo Cycles, Norman House, Hambridge Road, Newbury, Berkshire RG14 5XA, 01635 43186, www.banjocycles.com

HAMPSHIRE

village with a grandiose name. Great Bedwyn lies on the Kennet and Avon Canal, and the edge of the Savernake Forest, and what it lacks in size it more than makes up for in facilities. With direct rail links to Paddington, a fine pub and a Michelin-starred restaurant, not to mention numerous cycle trails such as the canal towpath and Wiltshire Cycleway on its doorstep, it would make a wonderful stop-over for bikepackers tending more towards the 'glamping' end of the camping spectrum.

For me though it was the beginning of my journey, and fresh off the train I rolled down the road that took NCN route 403 in a similar direction, past whitewashed cottages with low-slung thatched roofs. It took me less than a kilometre before I was off the beaten track, leaving waymarked routes behind in favour of hidden trails. A wide bridle path took me up to the edge of Foxbury Wood, but it wasn't long before I plunged into the wood, along a path that narrowed to the point of appearing impenetrable. Persevering through the knots of bramble and nettle, however, I emerged onto open byways. I could still feel the stings and abrasions on my limbs as I crossed a main road and headed past the hamlets of Shalbourne and Ham on flat, easy paths.

It had been the cycling equivalent of a stroll until now, although I had an idea of what awaited me as a waymarked Mid-Wilts Way fingerpost took me through wheat fields to the foot of an arduous climb between the Ham and Inkpen Hills. The grasses up the slope were waist-high in places, and the gradient was taxing enough to persuade me to push, up through gates into further crop fields, through which the beginning of a byway was shorn. Just a short while before I could barely make out any shift in the landscape at Bedwyn, the low hills little more than ripples in the landscape. Here, though, I was some 300 metres up at Inkpen

Beacon and could see far into Wiltshire and to the beginnings of Berkshire's Chiltern Hills, rolling away in the distance. It is up here, at Inkpen Beacon, that the Wayfarer's Walk begins and the Test Way from Southampton Water ends.

From here the former stretches 114 kilometres to the coast near Portsmouth, connecting with long distance paths at Emsworth (the Sussex Border Path) and Bedhampton (the Solent Way) en route. It also crosses three ancient routes (the South Hants and North Hants Ridgeways and the Harrow Way), where tracks were long ago worn into the land with the movement of animals, and transportation of salt and flint. The predominance of chalk in the landscape here has had a profound influence on it since time immemorial – traces of prehistoric man's hilltop earthworks can still be seen on the chalk ridges, the presence of which also means good arable and grazing land. And so it was that on my journey across the ridge I passed subtly shaded downland dotted with sheep and scattered with corn and barley fields, interspersed with beech trees and scrubland. The prevalence of flint too has shaped the villages near the downs, as I saw on countless cottages and churches on the early part of my ride, and here low flint walls ran unerringly alongside the path. The chalk pastures have helped a rich diversity of plants to flourish – from rock rose to kidney vetch – and though I know little of these things I could still identify different varieties of orchid that seem to thrive on the downs. I was surprised to recognise the songs of skylarks and cries of lapwings too.

At the site of an ancient fort atop Walbury Hill, the trail began to undulate before crossing a narrow road that ran down to Ashmansworth and ran alongside it, before peeling off over the main road into open downland shaped by ancient earthworks once more. As the trail traced a horseshoe

shape south then north, small copses of beech trees began to overhang the trail, while the steady drone of heavy traffic drifted to my ears. Within a few more kilometres I had reached the A-road that leads south to Adams' home in Whitchurch, while my quarry – his inspiration – lay on the other side. In his novel Adams had alluded to a dislike of motor transport, and its inherent danger to wildlife, and the rabbits that populated the warrens beyond this strip of tarmac were clearly as afraid of its dangers as their fictional brethren in *Watership Down*. Whereas I had until then seen neither hide nor hair of a rabbit along the Wayfarer's Walk, rising along the path that tunnels under the road, out onto Great Litchfield Down, I could see white tails bobbing and darting through the grass on all sides, and really began to feel as though I had wandered into the realms of Efrafa.

By now the light was beginning to fade, and I kept scanning the landscape ahead for possible places to pitch up for the night. Despite some perfect-looking nooks and hollows close to the trees, I was glad I held out, as the thinning path took me through a small sheep pen, over a country lane and onto Watership Down itself. Where better to spend the night than the very warrens and downs that in fictional form had stayed with me since childhood? I was clearly not the first to have thought this way; as a light rain began to fall I wandered into the trees and found a wigwam constructed from fallen branches. It was just large enough to stretch my bivvy bag out inside, with only my feet protruding from the entrance, and positioned in such a way so as to look out over the downs that fell away to the north. I had kept unintentionally recalling snippets from the *Watership Down* film all day, and as I settled down for the

night they were coming with such alacrity, it was as if I was enjoying my own private screening. By the time I was almost asleep it was the mystical rabbit folk-hero El-Ahrairah who drifted through my thoughts, though I no longer questioned his spiritual implications in the way I had done as a child. Instead I listened as the hum from the main road was gradually overtaken by nature's nocturnal traffic in the woods around me, as sleep gradually overcame me.

Breakfast was a relaxed affair. There was no rush the next morning as my ride was close to its end, so I stayed for a while alone on the downs before eventually wandering up to a field where fences and horse jumps had been sculpted from the hedges, before saddling up and heading south through a hollowed-out path through the trees. My route took me from quiet lanes to paths running through the last of the chalk downs' barley fields, which began to encroach on either side until the crop was brushing against my bars and elbows. Then woodland rose at the edge of the field and this last section before the road into Overton was an unexpected sliver of singletrack through the trees that begged to be ridden as quickly as my laden bike would allow.

At the station I had time to replay my passage along hedgerow, through woodland and down, and to think how a long ride or walk away from the roads can help you appreciate all the more how the passage of time can shape a landscape. This small stretch, moulded by ancient earthworks and decorated by flint constructions, coppices and arable land, certainly inspired Richard Adams; just as my passage across the country continued to inspire me in a myriad of ways, as unique as the landscape itself.

PART 1

PART 2

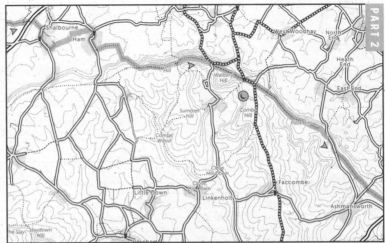

PART 3

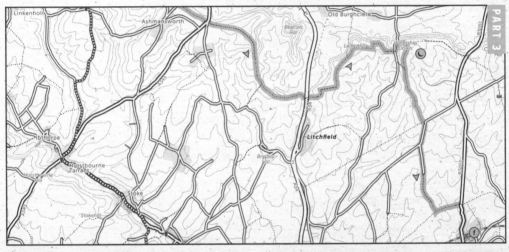

WONDER WEALD

A SURPRISING WEALTH OF TRAILS AWAIT THOSE EXPLORING KENT'S COASTAL FLATS AND ROLLING UPLANDS

The trails and paths that run across the rolling Kent Downs like veins have long been overlooked by mountain bikers in the south, many of whom are often lured by the promise of more dynamic riding along the South Downs, Chilterns, Surrey Hills and the western edge of the North Downs. However, not all of Kent is as flat as you think, particularly where the Kent Downs rise up out of the coastal flats and carry the North Downs Way along a ridge that stretches west as far as Farnham.

It's along the North Downs Way that a friend and I looked to travel deep into the heart of Kent. Part of this long-distance off-road ridge path follows the old Pilgrims Way, trod for hundreds of years by travellers from Winchester to the shrine of St Thomas Becket at Canterbury. Large parts are footpaths only, but the section around Wye has one of the longer stretches of bridleway. This seemed the ideal place from which to start a Kent adventure ride.

We stepped off the train at Wye, a typically picturesque Kentish village nestled on the fringe of the Kent Downs. Checking the map, it quickly became apparent that we would be off-road and climbing in no time. We spun out of the village at a fair rate in a bid to warm cramped muscles and began to head north-west, where a byway took

---

INFO:

START/FINISH: Wye station, Bridge Street TN25 5EB, 51.186142, 0.930086

DISTANCE: 32.4 miles/52.2km   **ASCENT:** 3008ft/917m   **OFF-ROAD:** 75%

TERRAIN: Chalky bridle paths and byways, woodland trails and quiet country lanes, with some busier roads towards Faversham. Climbs are occasional but testing.

NAVIGATION: Fairly easy. The bridleways along the North Downs Way are well signposted. Beyond Graveney, as the bridleway rises to crest the hill near Oversland, it is easy to miss a partially obscured sign which points you through a residential garden onto saturated pasture with dense woodland beyond. OS Landranger 179 is helpful.

EAT AND DRINK:

The Freewheel, Head Hill Road, Graveney, Kent ME13 9DE, 01795 538143, www.thefreewheel.pub

The White Lion, Selling, Kent ME13 9RQ, 01227 752742, www.shepherdneame.co.uk

SLEEP:

The Old Alma, Canterbury Road, Chilham, Kent CT4 8DX, 01227 731913, www.theoldalma.co.uk

Camp: Painters Farm, Painters Forstal, Faversham, Kent ME13 0EG, 01795 532995

Bivvy: Scoggers Hill

PROVISIONS:

Badgers Hill Farm, New Cut Road, Chilham, Kent CT4 8BW, www.badgershillfarm.co.uk

The Bike Warehouse, 32 Preston Street, Faversham ME13 8PE, 01795 539439, www.thebikewarehouse.net

white conical roofs making them easy to make out. More common here than anywhere else in the country, they speak of Kent's brewing heritage and have become emblematic of the county. Hops would have been spread out on the upper floors and dried by a wood-fired kiln (or *kell* in the Kentish dialect) below. The cowls that we could see still turning were used to let the heat escape. Now hops are dried industrially, but the oast houses here remain as wonderful examples of vernacular architecture.

We sailed through Selling as we lost height, riding through pasture and grazed meadows before joining a rough bridleway that runs parallel to the motorway, shielded by a row of stout ash trees. As we entered the southern fringe of Faversham, we stopped for a while to explore the market town, seeking out Abbey Street, one of the finest examples of a medieval thoroughfare in England. This street hosts the oldest market in Kent, and is mentioned in the Domesday Book. The sun was hanging low and heavy over our shoulders, so we decided to press on towards Goodnestone and Graveney in the hope of finding a good spot to camp. We were just wondering whether we had enough time to find a camping spot along the shore down at Seasalter, a few miles off our route, when we come across a remarkable little business in Graveney. It's evident immediately that this place – part pub, part café, part bike workshop – welcomes cyclists; what is not so immediately obvious is how warm that welcome will be. We popped in just to have a nose around, and before we knew it, we were sitting at the bar with a pint of Canterbury's finest pale ale, having been offered the pub garden for the night. While far from the wild camping I had planned, it appealed to us both as we realised just how weary the day's hill climbing had made us.

us through a ramshackle farmyard and rapidly up onto Soakham Downs. We were on the North Downs Way before we knew it, cutting through King's Wood before emerging onto open chalk downs, invaded by scrub.

The opening salvo of slopes were satisfyingly steep, but fortunately for us the downs began to undulate more gently as we passed through Shottenden and Perrywood. There are a number of unusual plants that thrive in the chalk earth here – dropwort and horseshoe vetch, and every once in a while a patch of orchids, endemic to the Kent hills.

As we rode closer towards Faversham, where the plains reach out towards the Swale estuary, a typically Kentish scene began to unfold around us. Hop fields and orchards reached out in the distance, punctuated by the occasional oast house standing like a sentry over the crops, their

It's often such unexpected turns that help define these two-wheeled adventures.

With the tent up we set about exploring our surroundings. The garden is lined with ancient bike frames, the interior full of cycling photos and memorabilia – I particularly liked the repurposing of old saddles and wheel rims for lampshades. Unsurprisingly the owner is a cycling buff who took the risk of reopening this dilapidated old pub along a popular Kent cycle club run. He's done it lovingly too, and listened to the residents to provide the proper pub they'd been yearning for. It hosts film nights and bike jumbles, and as we tucked in to jacket spuds later that night, a pianist played old standards to a packed house in what is normally the bike workshop. As he ended the evening with a rousing rendition of 'Roll Out The Barrel' – joined by audience and bar staff alike – we retired for the night, grinning at the unforeseen but most welcome hospitality we had stumbled upon. The chef even came in early the following morning to rustle up coffee and bacon sandwiches for us.

It's just as well we felt rested and refuelled, as we were climbing back onto the downs in no time. Before that, our route took us past the splendid Nash Court estate, a palatial-looking residence which was recently listed at auction for a trifling £2.5 million. We had to push our bikes along the wide path through fields past its lawns, and again on a footbridge a little further on over Boughton Street's bypass, but it did little to punctuate our progress. Our ascent continued on country lanes, and before long we'd left Graveney well behind in the mid-morning sunshine.

Soon we were riding through coppiced woodland, fresh stems sprouting from recently cut hornbeam, ash and sweet chestnut. The going was slow along a slim trail thick with nettles, but as we paused to take a breather our feet were quickly covered with voracious wood ants. A few formic acid-laced bites were enough to send us on our way, and mercifully the trail widened and became firmer through a nature reserve before crossing the train tracks that would take us home later that afternoon.

We set out along bridleways that followed the path of the Great Stour, then ran alongside the railway embankment. Byways took us south along grassy open downland, and then east, dropping back down into Wye. This village is well-appointed where pubs are concerned, and another warm welcome greeted us as we indulged in a post-ride pint. Not only had Kent supplied us with a challenging trail that had surpassed our expectations, but I couldn't help but feel that this county may be one of the best destinations for off-road riding near London.

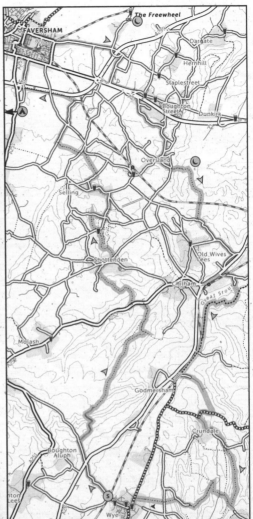

BIGNOR

NOVIOMAGUS

LONDINIUM

SUTTON

SLINDON

THE BEAUTIFUL SOUTH

SPECTACULAR VIEWS OF SEA AND WEALD FOLLOW THIS WEST SUSSEX SOJOURN FROM START TO FINISH

The newest of England and Wales' 13 designated National Parks, the South Downs is surprisingly one of the largest too. With only the Yorkshire Dales, Snowdonia and the Lake District covering a larger area, the South Downs National Park stretches over 1,600 square kilometres (over twice the area of the South Downs chalk range themselves, including large parts of the Weald). Running across its length, from Winchester to Eastbourne runs the South Downs Way, one of the few long-distance paths that can be ridden in its entirety. Because of this unusual accessibility, endurance riders have for years been drawn to the challenge of the 'SDW Double' – riding out along its 160km length, then back, in under 24 hours. The current record stands at 17h 47m 30s, which is remarkable when you consider the 3,810 metres of climbing involved before having to turn round and do it all again.

I rode the entire South Downs Way once, a few years ago, and was surprised how arduous the two-day transition from Winchester to Eastbourne

---

INFO:

START: Chichester railway station, Southgate PO19 8DL, 50.832069, -0.781692
FINISH: Arundel railway station, BN18 9PH, 50.847798, -0.546770

DISTANCE: 27.9 miles/45.0km   **ASCENT:** 3074ft/937m   **OFF-ROAD:** 85%

TERRAIN: Mostly chalk doubletrack, with occasional grassy bridleways and muddy forest tracks. Four or five significant climbs punctuate a ride that is rarely flat.

NAVIGATION: Fairly simple. Follow NCN route 2 then regional route 88 to Mid Lavant. Here the West Sussex Literary Trail north is only marked as a bridleway. Both the New Lipchis Way and South Downs Way are well signposted. There are a wealth of signed bridleways east of Amberley to chose from but you'll need OS Landranger 197 to navigate these well. The easier option is the riverside bridleway along from Houghton to Offham, which you can pick up opposite the George and Dragon pub.

EAT AND DRINK:

The George & Dragon, Houghton, Arundel, West Sussex BN18 9LW, 01798 831559, www.thegeorgeanddragonhoughton.co.uk
The Black Rabbit, Mill Road, Arundel, West Sussex BN18 9PB, 01903 882828, www.theblackrabbitarundel.co.uk

SLEEP:

Gumber Bothy, Gumber Farm, Arundel, West Sussex BN18 0RN, 01243 814484, www.nationaltrust.org.uk/slindon-estate
Bivvy: Coombe Wood, near Amberley

PROVISIONS:

St Martin's Coffee House, 3 St Martins Street, Chichester, West Sussex PO19 1NP, 01243 786715, www.organiccoffeehouse.co.uk
Hargroves Cycles, 106-108 The Hornet, Chichester, West Sussex PO19 7JR, 01243 537337, www.hargrovescycles.co.uk

SUSSEX

was. On that occasion I stayed at Gumber Bothy, a converted flint barn on a working sheep farm within the National Trust's Slindon estate. I rode back to explore the area once again, having been blind to the wonderful views down to Chichester and Arundel on my last visit, as the first leg from Winchester had taken so long darkness had fallen long before we reached the bothy. This time, with rail access from both Sussex towns providing the opportunity to explore this bite-sized chunk of the South Downs Way at my leisure, I could set up an overnight camp wherever I liked on the chalk ridge without having to race against fading daylight.

NCN route 2, then Regional route 88, whisked me away from Chichester's congested streets in no time, and before long I had left the clamour of road and rail traffic far behind, passing college games fields that were already a hive of activity despite the early hour. It made me think of the competitive nature of those cross-country riders that hare along the SDW in a bid to break the double record – I am in awe of the fitness, skill and

stamina of those men and women, yet I couldn't help feeling they are missing a trick. The chalk bridleways up on the Downs are wide enough to make night riding a possibility, but in doing so much of the beauty of the South Downs and all that they reveal must elude them. My foray was more of a leisurely one, rolling north along an old railway line from Chichester before crossing to the River Lavant's east bank and leaving the town suburbs behind. I coasted across peaceful pasture along the West Sussex Literary Trail, an 89km walking route with large stretches of bridle path from Horsham to Chichester Cathedral. This is a route alive with literary connections – from William Blake and John Keats to Percy Bysshe Shelley and Hilaire Belloc.

Nearing the famous Goodwood racecourse, I could make out the pronounced ridge of the Downs, sprawling across the horizon under a mottled canopy of greens, umbers and ochres, from Glatting Beacon in the east to Beacon Hill in the west. Whichever way I chose I'd have had to climb to 250 metres to meet the ridge so I skirted quickly through the busy village of Singleton before heading out onto undulating open downs, along the New Lipchis Way. This is another popular walking route, and takes the least arduous path up to the ridgeline of a handful of parallel tracks. The 200 metre ascent stretches out over three kilometres, first over exposed grassland then amid the confines of Singleton Forest, a low but steady gradient that left my breathing laboured as the first familiar South Downs Way fingerpost came into view. The ridge drops sharply to the north here; climbing the Downs from the coast tends to be the easier option. The next 15 kilometres or so promised to be wide, smooth flowing double-track, with expansive views once I left the woods of Graffham Down behind. Sure enough, the soft,

rutted trail soon firmed as the trees thinned out along Littleton Down. I began to recall details of my last visit here. In fading twilight I had raced down this slippery limestone track to meet the road, forced to climb the other side on equally fading legs. I also remembered the silhouette of a tiny Norman church standing alone in a field; now in broad daylight I could make out its tall, narrow nave and rounded chancel – a remarkable building that has changed little in almost 900 years. Only as I began the ascent to Glatting Beacon was I rewarded with the expansive views I'd so hoped for. Looking back over the chalk downland I surveyed farmsteads, hamlets, even entire parishes nestled between a patchwork quilt of rolling fields. Shafts of sunlight glinted off the bay by what must be Bognor Regis.

Dropping steeply off the ridge I found that farm traffic had turned the trail over Westburton Hill into an uphill slog. While not quite a quagmire, it was just sticky enough to adhere to anything it touched – tyres, frame, fork or feet – adding extra heft to an already-laden bike. At the crest of the hill any mud clearance I had was clogged up by this toffee-like mud. The effort failed to yield any reward downhill either; under the excess weight the bike's manoeuvrability became unpredictable, and at times I felt like I was aquaplaning down the slope. By the time I got to Coombe Wood I was exhausted and a rest stop at an old red-brick ruin amongst the trees turned into a permanent camp. Soon my hammock was up, steam rising from my stove, and my kit was spread out in the clearing as I prepared for nightfall. I wandered back to the track to watch the sun's last rays illuminate the sheer chalk cliffs beyond the Arundel-Amberley railway line and cast a warm glow over the Littlehampton shoreline, before retreating back to camp.

The next morning, as I rounded Amberley to negotiate the steep, technical trails along Perry Hill down to my journey's end in Arundel I thought I would only change two things – instead of crossing the River Arun I'd only go as far as Houghton, then drop down to a fantastic slice of riverside singletrack that runs all the way to Offham, by which time you can see the ramparts of Arundel's famous castle across the river. And I would put my winter tyres on, even though it was July.

This was the perfect UK adventure ride, and would be particularly good for the inexperienced rider. With towns and rail links at either end, it gives you a taste of wild ridgeline riding and camping without being at all remote. I took pleasure in the knowledge that even in such populated areas as the Sussex coast you could discover the bliss of the backcountry, countless miles rolling beneath your wheels without passing a soul.

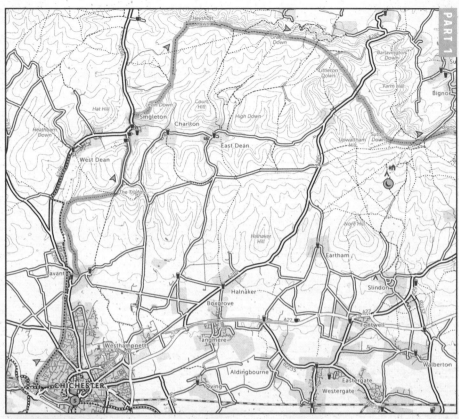

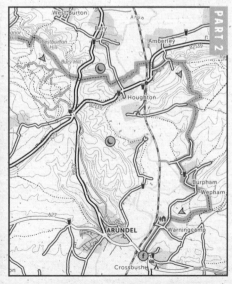

SANCTUARY ON THE SOLENT

THE ISLE OF WIGHT HARBOURS A WEALTH OF FOREST SINGLETRACK, AND HOLDS TRUE TO ITS PROMISE OF CONTINUAL COASTAL VIEWS

I zipped my down jacket right up as I stepped out on deck. The warmth of the late spring sun I had enjoyed on my ride down through the New Forest quickly evaporated as I was buffeted by a brisk sea breeze on board the Isle of Wight ferry. I was awaiting its departure from Lymington Pier on a half-hour-long voyage across the Solent, where a wealth of trail riding awaited me. I had expected the crossing to be busy, but nowhere near as much as it was. And what a well-heeled crowd too – every other person looked dressed up as if they were off to the races at Ascot. It was only when I got chatting

to one of the dolled-up day-trippers that I realised there was an event of some significance going on in Yarmouth, the ferry's destination and the beginning of my island micro-adventure. It turned out my visit coincided with the port's annual Old Gaffers Festival, a weekend of traditional 'gaff-rigged' (four-cornered) sail boat racing that was in its 19th year.

As we arrived in Yarmouth and I readied my bike by the loading doors, I could hear that the festival was already in full swing. It was certainly a colourful spectacle that greeted me as I rolled off the gangway and through the port, with a craft

---

INFO:

START/FINISH: Yarmouth ferry terminal, Quay Street PO41 0PB, 50.707250, -1.4998783

DISTANCE: 26.5 miles/42.6km   **ASCENT:** 2900ft/884m   **OFF-ROAD:** 75%

TERRAIN: Mostly wide chalky bridleways and forest tracks. All but the final climb are modest in gradient, with the toughest saved for last.

NAVIGATION: Fairly straightforward. Look out for NCN Route 22 signs to Wellow on leaving Yarmouth. NCN Route 231 will guide you back to the ferry from Freshwater. After crossing the road between Brighstone Forest and Shalcombe Down ignore a right turn then the left 100m on; instead continue to climb a steep chalky bridleway to the golf course. OS Landranger 196 covers the whole of this ride.

EAT AND DRINK:

The Bargeman's Rest, Little London Quay, Newport, Isle of Wight PO30 5BS, 01983 525828, www.bargemansrest.com
The Sun Inn, Hulverstone, Isle of Wight PO30 4EH, 01983 741124, www.sun-hulverstone.com

SLEEP:

YHA, Hurst Hill, Totland Bay, Isle of Wight PO39 0HD, 0845 371 9348, www.yha.org.uk
Camp: Chine Farm, Military Road, Ventnor, Isle of Wight PO38 2JH, 01983 740901, www.chine-farm.co.uk
Bivvy: near viewpoint at Limerstone Down

PROVISIONS:

Off The Rails, Station Road, Yarmouth, Isle of Wight PO41 0QT, 01983 761600, www.offtherailsyarmouth.co.uk
Wight Mountain, 31 Orchard Street, Newport, Isle of Wight PO30 1JZ, 01983 533445, www.wightmountain.com

fair, continental market, flower festival and classic vehicle display all part of the action too.

I could still hear the Bavarian brass band, who had been playing in the beer tent, long after I'd left the port behind, spinning out of town and onto country lanes in no time. Gradually the commotion receded and at the pretty village of Wellow, where every other thatched cottage seemed to have a cart or stall and honesty box for selling home-grown produce, a slow, steady ascent through lush green fields began. The more I climbed up the chalky downland, so typical of the island, the more spectacular the views that opened up behind me: between Yarmouth and the salt marshes and mudflats around Newtown Bay, the Solent was awash with vessels of every conceivable size, shape and colour. And across the strait my port of origin – Lymington – lay shimmering in the distance.

At Shalcombe I glanced around one more time to take in the scene before the scrub and cowslip gave way to the corner of Brighstone forest, which would form the backbone of my journey both to and from Newport. It was cool and quiet along the bridleway that skirted along the forest edge, but as wider, firmer trails took me deeper into its midst, I set off up a steepening trail into the heart of the forest, the southern edge of which formed the ridge along which the trail would take me home the following day, and where open downs offered far-reaching views over Brighstone, along Freshwater's white cliffs to the Needles rising out of Alum Bay and out into the Channel. Riding through Westover Plantation I felt cocooned along the shadowy bridle paths that looked as though they'd been hollowed by giant hands out of the forest.

I veered off the waymarked trails to enjoy secret little stretches of singletrack, but gradually, as I continued east, the paths widened into what

I presumed were old logging trails, the trees cut back to a respectful distance, and a dry, dusty chute propelled me down from my vantage point – though I hadn't realised how much height I had gained before I shot out of the trees halfway down the hill between Newbarn Down and Rowborough Down. This was the Tennyson Trail, which sent me careering down towards Carisbrooke and into the town of Newport. Having been here once before, I sought out the familiar stretch north of the town, where the River Medina flows up to Cowes and into the Solent, and where cafés are two a penny on the quay.

As I sat beneath the awning of a busy little place looking up the river, I pored over my maps, to look for something I had been meaning to locate for a while. Without a magnifying glass, though, it would be hard to decipher the encrypted cartographical code I had been told can be found on many an OS map – and on the Isle of Wight's cliffs and forests in particular. Apparently, it seems, cartographers can be a subversive bunch, prone to putting their own stamp on the contours of the land. I didn't have much joy with the flare of the early evening sun catching my eyes, but on my return home I noticed two such names worked cunningly into the cliffs (look carefully on the Landranger map under Warren Farm at SZ 314849 [50.663378, -1.556387], and near Blackgang at SZ 485776 [50.594109, -1.315491], for the names Trevor and Bill respectively).

I needed to find a camp for the night, and I still had to climb back onto Brighstone Down or nearby Limerstone Down if I wanted a 'room with a view'. The lanes south of Newport whisked me back to the foot of the downs, and as a gradual climb winched me over fields and out of Gatcombe, I could see hovering birds circling lazily over the exposed scrub, which looked for all the

world like buzzards. I had been told I might catch a glimpse of some on the island, along with its shyer residents, the adder and red squirrel, and before nightfall I'd been lucky enough to see both, lurking not far from the trig point on Limerstone Down. It was here that I headed to for the night, slinging my hammock between boughs at the forest's edge, which offered some respite from the rapidly cooling evening sea breeze. As the shadows lengthened I lit a small fire and wrapped up warm to watch the last of the sun's rays casting a brief golden glow over the fields before me, making silhouetted stacks of the Needles out in the bay.

When I woke the next morning, a weak sun was struggling to burn through a morning mist that had rolled up the bank from Brighstone. I was a little disappointed that my morning view had been lost behind this hazy filter, so I decided to ride on, re-joining the Tennyson Trail on the edge of Brighstone Forest. The sky remained burnt out, the atmosphere silent and muffled, and it was as if the glorious skies of the day before were already a distant memory. It was difficult to see where the white cliffs ended and the sky began, and even

the rolling chalk trail rising ahead of me seemed a rending split in the grassland, through which the sky could be seen.

All morning I had been riding on the periphery of the forest, parallel to and just a dozen metres apart from the track that had brought me here the day before, but a steep chalk bank south of Shalcombe took me into uncharted territory. It was only at the sight of the first bunker that I realised I was on a golf course atop East Afton Down. I'd been led to believe these downs would be a riot of colour at this time of the year, but I could only make out a muted palette of yellow-wort and knapweed beyond the fairway. Dropping down to the suburban outskirts of Freshwater, I was soon out on a straight, narrow causeway along Freshwater Marsh, which over my final few kilometres began to bleed into the River Yar. Other, more distant sounds overlapped the call of reed and sedge warblers along this nature trail – a rhythmic and harshly metallic intrusion, coming from the direction in which I was headed. There was no mistaking the Old Gaffers Festival's oompah band again, which I could hear along with their intoxicated audience long before I was within sight of the makeshift canvas music venue.

Judging by the state of some of the revellers I saw as I passed, I got the impression that the party hadn't ceased since I'd arrived the day before. Beyond the vessels moored nearby, the masts of other gaff-rigged boats were too numerous to count. Though the fine weather was short-lived and that morning's views muted, the splash of spring colour I had hoped to find on the island's beautiful chalk downs turned out to be waiting for me at the ferry port, on the sails and bunting bedecking each and every vessel. 'When in Rome', I thought, noting that my return ferry had yet to arrive, and headed into the raucous beer tent.

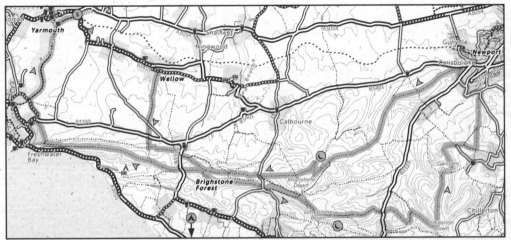

STANE STREET REVISITED

FAST FLOWING SINGLETRACK AMONG THE SURREY HILLS AND A WELL-PRESERVED ROMAN ROAD FORM THE BACKBONE OF THIS PICTURESQUE RIDE FROM THE NORTH DOWNS TO EPSOM DOWNS

For me the element of discovery is the key to bikepacking. Each ride is a journey, a potential adventure, and can yield unexpected rewards. And often there is a story imprinted in the landscape through which you travel, waiting to be told. Often these can be found in the traces of ancient trails that can still be found if you look closely, which speak of humanity's millennia-old movements across the land.

Having stumbled upon the remains of a Roman road near Amberley on the South Downs – called Stane Street from the Old English stān, referring to the stone surface – I was surprised to see the same name on a road sign at the start of my ride through the Surrey Hills, some 35 kilometres away on the western edge of the North Downs. Having left Ockley Station to tackle Leith Hill, the highest point in the South East, I noticed the name along the main road through the village, running north-north-east towards London, the same direction the Stane Street in West Sussex had travelled. Stane Street must be a common name for a Roman Road, I surmised.

INFO:

START: Ockley station, Capel RH5 5HT, 51.151641, -0.335752
FINISH: Epsom station, KT19 8EU, 51.333515, -0.269759

DISTANCE: 24.3 miles/39.1km   **ASCENT:** 3047ft/929m   **OFF-ROAD:** 80%

TERRAIN: Mostly muddy bridleways and rutted byways, with wooded singletrack on Leith Hill. Stane Street tends to be hard-packed or stony in most places. Very hilly to begin with, gradually flattening after Box Hill along Stane Street.

NAVIGATION: Mostly straightforward. The Greensand Way and Stane Street are waymarked routes and well signposted. At Leith Hill Tower descend on the main path (not the first, which is the Summer Lightning black run) and turn left at the junction along the Greensand Way. Under the railway bridge before White Down don't take the steep bridleway that doubles back up the hill; continue on to take the byway at Landbarn Farm. Use OS Landranger 187.

EAT AND DRINK:

The Tree on Boxhill, Box Hill, Tadworth, Surrey KT20 7PS, 01737 845996, www.thetreeboxhill.co.uk

The Prince of Wales, Guildford Road, Westcott, Dorking, Surrey RH4 3QE, 01306 889699, www.princeofwalesdorking.co.uk

SLEEP:

YHA, Radnor Lane, Holmbury St Mary, Surrey RH5 6NW, 0845 371 9323, www.yha.org.uk

Polyapes Scout Camp, Blundel Lane, Stoke D'Abernon, Cobham, Surrey KT11 2SL, 01372 842880, www.polyapesscoutcamp.ork.uk

Bivvy: Ashcombe Wood, Ranmore Common

PROVISIONS:

Leith Hill tower kiosk, www.national-trust.org.uk

Nirvana Cycles, 5 Guildford Road, Westcott, Surrey RH4 3NR, 01306 740300, www.nirvanacycles.com

It was only when I returned home that I discovered they are parts of the same ancient highway, a military road first used almost 2,000 years ago that connected London to the military and naval supply base at Chichester. Although some parts have now become metalled major roads, you can follow a trace of footpaths and byways on a map that still form an almost continuous line between its points of origin. At no point along its 90km length does it veer more than 10km from a direct line between London Bridge and Chichester; if it weren't for the steep crossings of the North and South Downs and Greensand Ridge it probably wouldn't have veered from its course at all.

Later in my journey on toward the famous racetrack at Epsom I would traverse a significant portion of the well-preserved stretch between Box Hill and Thirty Acres Barn near Ashtead, now listed as a Scheduled Monument, but for now my mind was on other things. Only a few kilometres into my ride, along a quiet, leafy lane to Forest Green, my route headed north and began its steep but steady progress toward the crest of Leith Hill. My arrival at the tower, which stands 294 metres above sea level, would herald fine views across the Low Weald and North Downs, but it looked like I would have to earn that reward and those on offer in the tower's miniature café. It was a steep grind up past Leith Hill

Place, the former home of Ralph Vaughan Williams, but having at last found my rhythm on the climb I was reluctant to stop.

As the road skirted around the foot of Leith Hill I latched on to the Greensand Way, a wide, muddy bridle path that had become a slippery bed of amber leaves. It was a surprisingly easy route to the top, but only gave me glimpses of the height I'd gained through the trees, raising the curtain on the finest views in the South East only when the tower appeared over the brow. Over a much needed mug of tea I soaked up the scene, and could make out not only my point of arrival this morning down along Stane Street but also, hazy beyond Dorking, Leatherhead and the tarmac confines of the M25, my destination of Epsom Downs.

I know this area well, and arriving at Epsom would transport me back to the town I knew in my school days. Younger still, I was once convinced we went for weekend walks on 'Ups and Downs'; reality, when it eventually dawned, was something of a disappointment. My first forays into mountain biking were up these hills too – I would revisit Leith Hill, Box Hill and Ranmore Common, but Holmbury Hill and Pitch Hill are a little further west – and the 10km or so from my descent off Leith Hill would be something of a nostalgia trip. My bike was too overburdened to attempt the Summer Lightning trail that drops off the top; the full-face helmets of the downhillers that hurled themselves down off the trailhead told me all I needed to know. Instead I rejoined the Greensand Way, which follows the ridge of greensand rock across Surrey and Kent, twisting 174km from Haslemere to Romney Marsh and the Kent coast. It was a pleasant, gradual descent, through falling leaves, and it was worth the slog across an adjacent byway chewed up by motocross bikes to find a lovely singletrack descent I remembered well into the village of Westcott, the

great little bike shop there a regular pit stop for me over the years. The staff offered to look after my burdensome kit, so I headed off back the way I had come, with plenty of time to clear the descent before the shop closed.

Back at the tower I followed hot on the heels of a lad on a long-travel full suspension machine, who careened off down the slope. Although he soon left me for dust as I gingerly approached one drop-off after another on my rigid steel frame, I had an absolute blast, swooping round bermed corners and rocketing down a root-strewn chute. I shot back out into Westcott with a broad grin on my mud-splattered face and returned to the shop to gather my kit and set off up to Ranmore Common. It's here that I spent the night, rather than further up the trail, and a push up the steep bridle path that runs across the slope to meet the Pilgrim's Way up on White Down gave me plenty of opportunity to scout out the woods for a camp site.

A clearing just off the trail looked down into Dorking and offered shelter from a chill breeze that I could suddenly feel. It looked like the perfect spot, though I was glad I had the tent's protection rather than just a simple tarp shelter. It was hidden well enough for me to justify building a small fire, and there was ample dry dead wood and tinder nearby. With the tent up and a fire crackling nicely, I listened to the sounds drifting up the hill from Dorking – the drone of traffic, the rattle of occasional trains and briefly a piercing siren. It was an unfamiliar perspective of a very familiar place, a wild camp once again adding a new dimension to my journey. I would strike out the next morning along a trail that would be entirely new to me, though it's older than the towns it passes.

When I eventually arrived along the hoof-pitted bridleways that stretch over Epsom Downs, leading me over the racecourse and past the grandstand, childhood memories came flooding back. Every

aspect of 'Ups and Downs' was just as it had been, and my journey here from the mountain bike haunts of my twenties to the town of my school days felt like a trip back in time. I noticed a similar feeling after passing the 120-year-old fort on Box Hill now inhabited only by bats, then rolling down the ancient chalky byway of Stane Street, rumbling over the preserved stony sections that gave it its name. Along that quiet corridor my mind was flung further back to a time when the road wasn't silent, forgotten and overgrown but felt the constant tread of human traffic.

Stane Street is a road I'd like to ride all the way and, as I'm learning as my adventure rides take me greater distances, there is always a network of trails across the British countryside with which to take any ride away from the road along paths less travelled. The next time I pass through here, I thought as I boarded a train home at Epsom, will be on a journey not completed in its entirety for countless years – following long-disappeared wheel tracks of traders trekking from Chichester to London Bridge. That's the great thing about adventure rides, I noticed; each one tends to inspire another, often longer, further afield and a little more ambitious. And at the heart of every one lies that ever-present desire – for discovery.

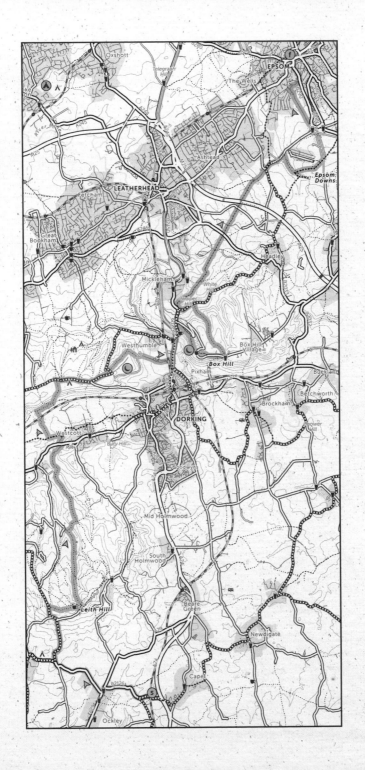

MIDLANDS & NORTH

FROM FEN TO FOREST

A ROMAN ROAD STRETCHING INLAND FROM HUNSTANTON TO THETFORD PROVIDES A GREAT INTRODUCTION TO ADVENTURE BIKING

As a bikepacking route this is a perfect introduction to adventure riding – that is, cycling off-road on trails that have evolved with the landscape, camping wild along the route with only the provisions you can carry with you, and immersing yourself in your natural surroundings. Many writers and painters have tried to capture the essence of the East Anglian landscape – the seemingly endless fields and dykes of the Fens and the yawning coastal mudflats of the Wash estuary. Perhaps writer and photographer Dominick Tyler came closest when he observed that "time and space are altered when you pass into those wide, flat lands". This otherworldliness beneath the fullest of skies is something I had hoped to experience for myself along the Peddars Way, an ancient route crossing Norfolk from the coast at Holme-next-the-Sea.

Continuing 76km in an almost unwavering plumb-line to cross the border into Suffolk at Knettishall Heath, it is the only waymarked route I followed from beginning to end for this book, but

---

INFO:

START: The White Horse, Kirkgate, Holme-next-the-Sea, Norfolk PE36 6LH, 52.960846, 0.537863
FINISH: Knettishall Heath Country Park, Knettishall, Thetford, Suffolk IP22 2TQ, 52.387969, 0.856749

DISTANCE: 45.6 miles/73.5km   **ASCENT:** 2463ft/750m   **OFF-ROAD:** 70%

TERRAIN: Stony bridleway, country lanes, minor roads, forest singletrack. Mostly flat and straight, slightly hillier and more technical towards Thetford Forest.

PUBLIC TRANSPORT: Harling Road station is just a mile detour if you cut the Peddars Way a few miles short and Thetford is 12km from the end at Knettishall Heath, if you wish to remain car-free.

NAVIGATION: Easy. The Peddars Way is waymarked from start to finish. There is a brief byway deviation that will take you off the route at Ringstead, where it becomes a footpath. So too at North Pickenham, where it is best to continue through the village, turn right onto Houghton Lane and right again to re-join the Peddars Way, avoiding a section of footpath and stiles through the fields near Meadow Farm. OS Landranger maps 132 and 144 cover the route.

EAT AND DRINK:

King William IV, Heacham Road, Sedgeford, Hunstanton, Norfolk PE36 5LU, 01485 571765, www.thekingwilliamsedgeford.co.uk
The Chequers Inn, Griston Road, Thompson, Thetford, Norfolk IP24 1PX, 01953 483360, www.thompsonchequers.co.uk

SLEEP:

The Ostrich Inn, Stocks Green, Castle Acre, Kings Lynn, Norfolk PE32 2AE, 01760 755398
Greenwoods Campsite, Old Fakenham Road, Tatterset, Norfolk PE31 8RS, 01485 528808, www.greenwoodscampsite.co.uk
Bivvy: fields west of Castle Acre

PROVISIONS:

Bircham village store, Bircham Riad, Great Bircham, Kings Lynn, Norfolk PE31 6RJ, 01485 576006
Fat Birds, 12 Kings Lynn Road, Hunstanton, Norfolk PE36 5HP, 01485 535875, www.fatbirds.co.uk

in doing so I hoped to see and feel the landscape in a similar way to those who have trodden this path for nigh on 2,000 years. It may not be the wildest of places – not even Thetford Forest, which attracts walkers and cyclists in droves – but it is a timeless one. Believed to be a Roman road there is considerable conjecture that it is older still, and was only remodelled by the Roman occupation.

At Knettishall the Peddars Way joins the possibly prehistoric Icknield Way, which heads south for more than 160km to connect with the ancient Ridgeway at Ivinghoe Beacon in Buckinghamshire. It continues unerringly south-west to Avebury in Wiltshire, and further still along the Wessex Ridgeway to Lyme Regis in Dorset – together forming the Greater Ridgeway, an ancient track scoured across some 500km of countryside by the passage of beasts, carts and men. While its origins are unclear, the name can almost certainly be attributed to the Romans, coming from the Latin *pedester*, 'on foot', which is how the majority of its traffic across the millennia would have travelled.

As I prepared to set out, dozens of anglers were turning over the muddy sand with forks in the low-tide shallows along the coast of Hunstanton, searching for worms to bait their hooks. Before long I had left the dunes, cliffs and mudflats of Hunstanton and Holme behind, and I weaved

briefly round the village of Ringstead before the ancient drovers' road set its course south and east. Although to all intents and purposes the Peddars Way is a waymarked route, it never feels as such; more a series of forgotten byways that nature is gradually reclaiming. Bar a few complicated twists and turns around Castle Acre – the mid-way point and my camp for the night – it's a ride that negates the need for navigation. Instead it lets you soak up the scenery so typical of the border between Lincolnshire and Norfolk. The unyielding panorama is only punctuated by farmsteads, hamlets or the odd windmill. It encourages the eye to wander and follow its rolling expanse – not just a kilometre or so, but to the distant horizon. It can pass in a blur if you are so inclined, or can yield the most interesting details – field mice in the corn; a curlew or kite on the wing; a glimpse of a lapwing nesting amid the hedgerows or in the lanes' uncultivated edges (known as 'marfer' in these parts).

In the distance the purple gardens of Norfolk Lavender, and the magnificent estates of Houghton Hall (built by Britain's first Prime Minister Sir Robert Walpole) and Sandringham House slipped by as I rode along a path rutted and hard-packed, stony in places and hemmed in by high briar in others, but always presenting a taut ribbon stretching through seemingly unreachable horizons.

Past the church spires at Fring and Anmer and the route had barely risen 30 metres since the coast; by Harpley and both Little and Great Massingham, however, there was a noticeable tug as the gradient steepened. Along the final few miles into Castle Acre, the dirt track gives way, and it was almost startling after some 30km alone to be sharing the road again.

The village here is an ideal place to break the journey. At a junction between the Peddars Way and the River Nar, it harbours not only the remains of the

Norman fortifications that gave the village its name, but also a Cluniac Priory, now under the auspices of English Heritage. Evidence of its stature as a fortified town can be seen in its Bailey Gate. It looked all the more beautiful bathed in spring's evening glow as I arrived and made my way to the Ostrich Inn. The landlord at this handsome, red-bricked 16th century coaching inn tried to tempt me to take one of his spacious oak-beamed bedrooms for the night, but it was too glorious an evening to be hemmed in by walls. Instead I found a peaceful patch overlooking the town, where I could sit outside my tent, eat a simple supper and watch the sun set over the village's ruined castle walls.

An explanation for my restless night greeted me at first light; I unzipped the tent to find a blanket of frost lending a silver sheen to the grass and crystallizing the surface of my equipment. Glad to have bought a tent and sleeping bag liner rather than my usual bivvy and tarp kit, I still had to rub some feeling back into my toes and get a hot brew on the go, before deciding the best way to warm up would be to ride it out. Packed up and mounted within minutes I followed the familiar

Peddars Way markers out of the sleepy village, through South Acre and Bartholomew's 'Hills' – still little more than a mound – before the road once more yielded to dirt doubletrack, and birch copses became more commonplace. After dropping down into something of a basin, I was forced to shoulder the bike over stiles and footbridges at North Pickenham. It's the tarmac that prevails after that once more for a time, but because of the hour or the narrowness of the lanes they were devoid of traffic, and only as I passed another squat windmill at Little Cressingham did I see a car for the first time. There is a narrow bridle path that runs parallel to the road, separated by a thin veil of trees. The track veered off obliquely, which carried me into thickening woodland, deciduous at first before pine and conifer took over, as I left an MoD firing range behind and edged closer to Thetford Forest. Along wide forest trails I met the National Cycle Network's route 13 from Bury St Edmunds to Fakenham, but that too peeled off and disappeared as I rolled on south over quiet miles, on the cusp of dense forest and open heath.

I caught glimpses of other riders through the trees, of families picnicking in clearings, and dog walkers traipsing along other trails, but this pathway, trodden by countless feet before me, was disturbed by my wheels alone. Only as a boarded section took me over the wetlands of Blackwater and back into the trees did I once more see wanderers through the forest, ethereal nymph-like figures, who appeared in hazy spots of sunshine then vanished into shadow.

As I reached the end of the Peddars Way at Knettishall's meadows and grassland, I crossed these solitary plains. The number of travellers traversing this ancient route may well have dwindled to near non-existence, but those who do can't help but hear the echoes of a long lost past.

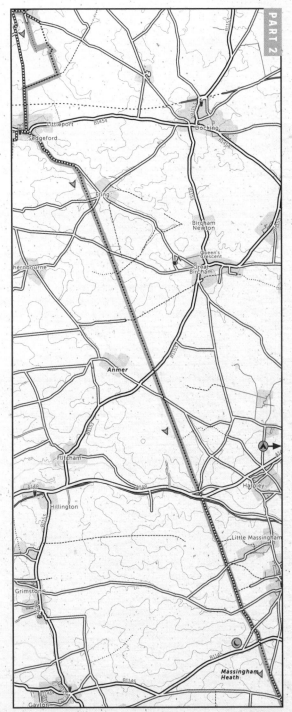

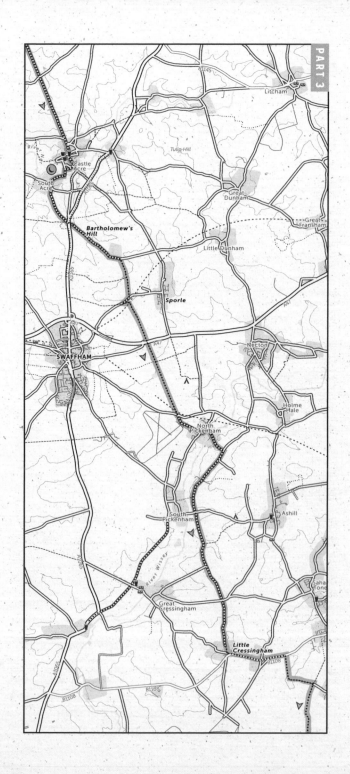

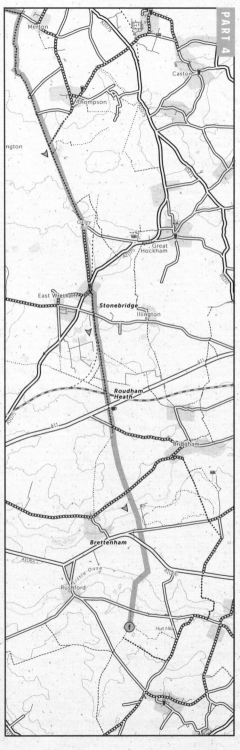

A DRIFT THROUGH WILD MIDLAND MEADOWS

THE VIKING WAY AND RUTLAND ROUND FORM THE SPINE OF A JOURNEY FROM BELVOIR VALE TO RUTLAND'S COUNTY TOWN

Very much like the Peddars Way further east, this route encompassing the Viking Way and Rutland Round is a fairly linear, undulating route that could easily be undertaken on a cross bike, rugged tourer or rigid hardtail. Having spent much time over the last ten years bemoaning the lack of mountain biking opportunities around the pancake-flat Fens, from where my wife hails, I began extending my horizons each time we'd visit, stumbling first upon the Peddars Way and latterly this route, a good day's ride south, from the quaint little village of Bottesford in Leicestershire to Oakham, in the heart of England's smallest county, Rutland.

Whether it's by design, coincidence or some latent inner desire, I often find my explorations by bike heading towards a large body of water (usually the coast), and this route fits the same mould. Though the body of water in question is considerably smaller, Rutland Water is still the largest man-made lake in England, and is blessed not only by picturesque rolling countryside but also by two bike shops along its shores, as well as numerous opportunities to indulge in water sports.

INFO:

START: Bottesford station, Station Road NG13 0GT, 52.946058, -0.793716
FINISH: Oakham station, Station Road LE15 6QT, 52.672513, -0.731974

DISTANCE: 31.2 miles/50.2km   **ASCENT:** 1404ft/428m   **OFF-ROAD:** 80%

TERRAIN: Rough, rutted bridleways, open fields and country lanes. An undulating route that feels flatter than it is.

NAVIGATION: Fairly simple. The Rutland Round and Viking Way are well signposted, and NCN Route 63 delivers you into Oakham. However, it is easy to lose the trail through Edmondthorpe Mere and Woodwell Head. Make sure you keep the fence and tree-line on your left as you head east. OS Landranger 130 covers most of the route, except for Oakham which can be found on 141.

EAT AND DRINK:

White Lion Inn, 38 Main Street, Whissendine, Rutland LE15 7ET, 01664 474233, www.whitelioninn.com
The Lord Nelson, 11 Market Place, Oakham, Rutland LE15 6DT, 01572 868340

SLEEP:

Cross Swords Inn, The Square, Skillington NG33 5HB, 01476 861132, www.thecross-swordsinn.co.uk
Rutland Caravan & Camping, Park Lane, Greetham, Oakham LE15 7FN, 01572 813520, www.rutlandcaravanandcamping.co.uk
Bivvy: Woodwell Head, near Teigh

PROVISIONS:

Zaro's, 12 Queen Street, Bottesford, Leicestershire NG13 0AH, 01948 843699
Giant Store Rutland Water, Normanton car park, near Edith Weston, Oakham, Rutland LE15 8HD, 01780 720888, www.giant-rutland.co.uk

I originally planned to start here and head north into Leicestershire, before realising that Bottesford is a bit of a rail outpost with irregular services; better to start there, I realised, and have a wider choice of trains (and pubs) at my disposal on reaching Rutland. Despite its apparent size and tranquillity, Bottesford is actually the largest village in the Vale of Belvoir, known for the Duke and Duchess of Rutland's vast manse, which dominates the skyline for miles around. Similarly, the spire of St Mary's church, the highest in Leicestershire at 212ft, was still visible four or five kilometres into my journey south. Leaving the village behind and crossing a busy main road, I was soon riding a barely visible bridleway that traversed grazing pasture before a track led me down through fields of blackening legumes towards the disused but pleasant Grantham Canal.

The 53km-long canal, which falls through 18 locks to join the River Trent at West Bridgford, had the grassy remnants of a towpath running alongside it, as well as a parallel dedicated cycle path. I opted for the solitude of the former and was rewarded by the sight of occasional cranes wading through the lilies and tall grasses along the canal banks, as well as a kite or two darting overhead. Belvoir Castle cut an imposing figure, high on its hill beyond the canal, and only disappeared when I veered off the towpath, crossed the canal on one of the many bridges made from dusky red local Bottesford brick, just after NCN routes 15 and 64 intersected, and began to climb up behind Cliff Wood to Woolsthorpe-by-Belvoir.

I was in what is the final section of the Viking Way, a 237km predominantly walking route that meanders from the Humber Estuary, through Lincoln and the Lincolnshire Wolds to Rutland Water. This section was all bridleway; occasion-ally cobbled or rutted red clay, but mostly a thin ribbon of singletrack that furrowed through silent stretches of wonderful wildflower meadows known as The Drift, or Sewstern Drift further south. This Site of Special Scientific Interest, where Saxon earthworks known as King Lud's Entrenchments can be found, contains some of the rarest wildflower-rich limestone grassland in the country. Such flowers as the wild mignon-ette, greater knapweed and ox-eye daisy can be seen here in abundance like nowhere else in the country. Skylarks, corn buntings and linnets too also populate the grassland, though their numbers across the country are declining.

It is hard to imagine what this stretch was like 150 years ago, dented with hoof marks of lowing cattle trailing southwards from Scotland or Yorkshire to the London slaughterhouses. There's evidence that it may even have been the oldest, pre-Roman route between the Stamford and Newark regions. I had the old road to myself; even when I emerged from the trees into a clearing where, beside cornfields, lay a tarmac airstrip, hangars and strange nautical-looking cases, up to ten metres long, lined up in neat rows alongside what looked like a club house. Indeed the Gliding Centre is one of the most popular gliding clubs in central England. While the only waymarked signs I could see up here were footpaths, my OS map clearly showed bridleway rights of way across the top of the landing strip. On another day it might pay to look out for turning aircraft before making a dash for the bridleway beyond the clubhouse, along which the Viking Way continues.

Soon the bridleway petered out and a road section took me around the villages of Sewstern and Buckminster – the closest the route came to opportunities for provisions until the outskirts of Oakham at Whissendine. A paved track running parallel to the road was whittled down to the

embellishments make al-fresco cooked food seem sumptuous. The evening was warm and mercifully dry, so I hooked my hammock up at the edge of the trees and it wasn't long before I was lulled to sleep by the silence that had fallen on the vale.

Eager to push on the next morning, I was packed and on the bike long before whatever passed for rush hour on the village roads got under way. I was not far beyond the sleepy hamlet of Teigh before a partially paved bridleway took me cross-country once more, over the railway line that runs into Oakham, and delivered me just outside Whissendine. The trail meandered over exposed, undulating fields, over which gusts of wind were beginning to whip in, before I found respite behind the high hedgerows along the road to Langham, the last conurbation before I reached my destination.

Langham was a bustling little place, and a shock to the system after so much solitude over the last 40km or so. The Rutland Round peeled off into Barleythorpe, but I made a beeline for Oakham along the NCN's route 63. I knew Rutland's county town well, but had never really considered it as offering much in the way of off-road adventures, and although my route hadn't presented much of a technical challenge, it had allowed me to cover a large swathe of countryside. Sometimes there's nothing more pleasing on a bike than feeling long stretches of trail disappear beneath your wheels. You see the countryside change, feel the weather shift – I even noticed a pronounced change in accent, with one friendly old boy at Bottesford doffing his cap to me and saying, "Ow do" with a strong Nottingham twang. With my journey done I had plenty of time to head a little out of town to soak up the splendour of Rutland Water and grab a little shut-eye on its grassy banks, before returning along the off-road trail that skirts the shore to the station.

now familiar rutted red clay-like byway, with deep water-logged gouges churned up, it seemed, by motorcross bikes. But as I passed the whinnying sounds of horses from nearby stables a short stretch of road along Drift Hill and Fosse Lane brought some relief. It was short-lived, however, as the Rutland Round quickly took me back over farmers' fields, initially a long, straight track shorn into the wheat stubble before hard-packed, pock-marked dirt tracks hugged the edges of the woods and skirted around a patchwork of further fields, affording fine views south over Market Overton, Barrow and beyond.

With evening fast approaching it was here, at Woodwell Head, that I stopped to make camp, with perhaps just a third of the 50km route left to cover the next day. I couldn't help but marvel at the silence that seemed to engulf me as the sun set – the A1 was mercifully far enough away to be no more than a distant hum, and apart from that it was just birdsong and the odd scurrying rabbit that offered the sole soundtrack to accompany my stove-cooked supper. I couldn't resist picking up slices of black pudding at a butcher in the Fens before I left, which I added to my satisfying stodge of sweet potato. Even the simplest of

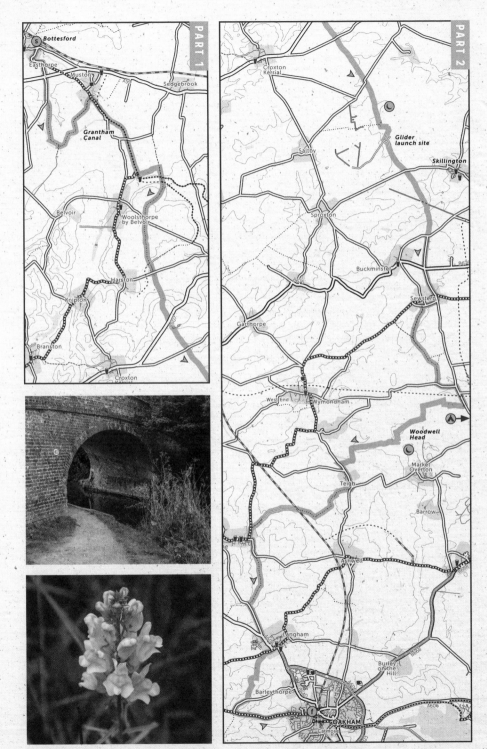

A WOLD AWAY

FROM THE COTSWOLD EDGE THE GOLDEN HEARTLANDS OF GLOUCESTERSHIRE ROLL AS FAR AS THE EYE CAN SEE

Choosing where to ride in the Cotswolds is like picking a sweet from a pick'n'mix tin – there is so much to choose from, each route a subtle variation on the rest, but every one ultimately rewarding. These are the heartlands of quintessential 'Englishness'; rolling hills and farmland, country manors and honey-coloured cottages, hedgerow-lined lanes and ancient oak trees. But behind the tea-and-scones facade of gentrified Cotswold life lies a community of mountain bikers who revel in the riding on their doorstep – Winchcombe, Ilmington, Bredon Hill, Wotton-under-Edge; look closely in the jam-like mud on any Cotswold trail and you'll see traces of fresh tyre tracks no matter what the season. Winchcombe Cycling Club even hosts its own version of the gruelling cobbled classic cycling race Paris-Roubaix. Instead of pavé, their endurance event, the 'Hell of the North Cotswolds', is ridden over the steep-sided muddied hills of the Cotswolds.

I've ridden around Winchcombe to the north-east of Cheltenham before, along a section of the Cotswold Way, but Birdlip to the south is new to me, and supposedly boasts one of the finest views in Gloucestershire at Barrow Wake, so it was here that I pointed my wheels after alighting at Cheltenham Spa train station on a glorious late spring morning.

INFO:

START / FINISH: Barrow Wake car park GL4 8JY, 51.840466, -2.098289

DISTANCE: 14.9 miles/24.0km   **ASCENT:** 1837ft/554m   **OFF-ROAD:** 75%

TERRAIN: Often muddy dirt bridleways, stony paths and narrow lanes. The steepest climbs occur when travelling up to the Cotswold Edge; after that the trail is undulating.

NAVIGATION: Fairly simple. It's a straightforward loop with well signposted bridleways and waymarked sections of the Cotswold Way. When leaving Birdlip along the B4070, be careful not to leave the treeline and head south to Hazel Hanger Wood; instead stay left to emerge from the trees at Blacklains Farm. Use OS Landranger 163.

EAT AND DRINK:

The Golden Heart Inn, Birdlip, Gloucestershire GL4 8LA, 01242 870261, www.thegoldenheart.co.uk

The Green Dragon, Cockleford, Cowley, Gloucestershie GL53 9NW, 01242 870271, www.green-dragon-inn.co.uk

SLEEP:

The Colesbourne Inn, Colesbourne, Gloucestershire GL53 9NP, 01242 870376, www.thecolesbourneinn.co.uk

Camp: Jackbarrow Farm, Duntisborne, Glos GL7 7LD, 07746 281872, www.jackbarrowcs.co.uk

Bivvy: on banks of River Churn, Coberley

PROVISIONS:

Primrose Vale Farm Shop, Shurdington Road, Bentham, Gloucestershire GL51 4UA, 01452 863359, www.primrosevale.com

Leisure Lakes Bikes, 27 Pittville Street, Cheltenham, Gloucestershire GL52 2LN, 01242 251505, www.leisurelakesbikes.com

It was a tough road climb to get to the start of the loop at Barrow Wake, an Iron Age burial site, but it was worth it. Both Cheltenham and neighbouring Gloucester's limestone-hewn houses glowed golden in the morning sun, rich verdant slopes and yellow fields of rape rolling away into the haze and the Vale of Evesham beyond.

From this superb vantage point I walked my way down the steepest slopes overlooking Little Witcombe, saddling up to ride a thin off-camber trail that followed the contours of the escarpment's lower reaches. Losing a little height at first gave me some perspective as I looked back at what's known as the Cotswold Edge, rising steeply from the meadows of the Upper Thames. It was good to put the hill between me and the busy A road, and to leave the viewpoint, around which milled day-trippers, dog walkers and Duke of Edinburgh Award students keenly studying their maps. The upper slopes were wooded, and past a small farm my path rose to the road at Birdlip and, although the paths through Witcombe Woods looked inviting, I knew I had to stick to the road for a while or I would miss a bridleway that runs away from the woods and out into open farmland.

The tracks and narrow country lanes that ushered me out through Brimpsfield and Elkstone were typical Cotswold fare, a painterly patchwork of cornfields and other arable land hemmed in by high hedgerow borders. An underpass beneath a main highway was the only interlude in an otherwise peaceful procession across crop fields, past brambles and thickets and along well-trodden bridlepaths, the ground pock-marked with many a horse's hooves. Before long the rivers Frome and Churn had disappeared beneath my wheels, the latter twice as the trail took me north at Colesbourne. The old coaching inn here made an ideal rest stop, allowing me time to savour the views

over the north Cotswolds from its peaceful garden. I didn't linger long though, as my thoughts turned to making good progress before seeking a camp for the night, though more immediately it was the climb to Upper Coberley that confronted me. I found plenty of traction along the well-worn grassy bridlepath that skirts around Pinswell Plantation. It dropped briefly to the road along the Gloucester Way, which crosses the width of the county from Chepstow to Tewkesbury, before climbing once and renewing my acquaintance with the Churn. It looked like open fields for the next few kilometres so, with the light fading, I found a spot along its wooded banks that was far away enough from the road, Coberley's church or any dwellings, and set up my shelter for the night.

As I sat by the River Churn, which here did little to live up to its name, running slow and clear, and in most places shallow, I scanned the waters for cray, hoping to liven up my pasta with a little crayfish meat. But the shallows showed no sign of marauding North American crays, or the smaller hapless natives which their cousins from across the 'Pond' are steadily driving from the rivers. All I caught were the radiating ripples – or 'wellums' – caused by surfacing fish in the river's deeper middle, though never the fish themselves. So my meal went ungarnished except for a little shredded wild garlic, though my evening down by this babbling brook was no less enjoyable for it. The church bells pealed for the last time as I pulled the drawstrings around both my sleeping bag and bivvy to keep the chill night air at bay.

I hadn't really stopped to check my position until over breakfast, and was surprised to find I was no more than half a dozen kilometres from the end of my journey. The going had been surprisingly easy on these firm tracks and trails. Cotswold mud is renowned for its stickiness, and

after even the shortest bout of rain the trails can become interminably heavy. I had been lucky, however: it had been dry for weeks now, and the sunlight had already started to filter through the canopy as I rolled up my dry-bags. The initial stretch out of Coberley followed a line of ash trees west for a while, with well-kept and covered horses looking nonchalantly up at me as I interrupted their grazing.

Then I was out onto dusty roads for a while, and climbed onto a thin bridle path that gradually disappeared, which is where things started to go awry. My GPS failed, leaving me groping uncertainly through fields trying to get back on track. I was in Coldwell Bottom, a steep-sided gulley, with no trace of a trail, so instead of pushing up either bank I ploughed on along the bottom through the scrub, only to meet a dead end where fences and hedgerows formed an effective and frustrating blockade. As I stood there, knee-deep in wild grasses, contemplating my next move, I made out some kind of antennae, poking out from the far trees. They could only be the aerial masts of Birdlip radio station on Shab Hill near Barrow Wake. I waded through the tall grasses to a point in the fence that looked breachable, and with renewed vigour tossed my bike over into the next field before squeezing between the briars to join it. Just as I found my bearings, my GPS signal belatedly returned, and it was only after I rode roughshod over ploughed fields to the farm at Shab Hill that I saw a right of way trail veering off ahead past kennels and Cuckoopen Farm – the trail I should have come down on but had somehow lost.

Choosing to blame the lack of waymarks rather than my navigational ability, I clambered back on and headed past the aerials and humming pylons towards the thrum of traffic, within minutes crossing the A-road and finding with relief a sign that pointed me in the right direction – that of the Cotswold Way. This firm, waymarked path guided me on to the end of my ride, that beautiful panorama upon Barrow Wake. This had been a ride that embodied all that is good about cycling in the Cotswolds, and there can't be many prettier places to get lost in.

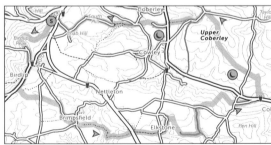

Nº.18

MALVERN'S GREAT SENTINEL

THE WILDEST OF CAMPS NEAR WORCESTERSHIRE'S HIGHEST PEAK OFFERS SPECTACULAR VIEWS OVER COUNTLESS COUNTIES

There's an immediate appeal to the town of Great Malvern, particularly for those stepping off the train, amid a leafy suburb to the east of the town. The wide, tree-lined avenues and handsome Victorian houses speak of a certain affluence – built on the back of the town's 19th century rise to prominence as a health resort – yet you'll find nothing but a friendly, down-to-earth welcome from the townsfolk here. And for those of an adventurous mind-set there is something of even greater innate appeal – in the heart of this Area of Outstanding Natural Beauty lies a huge crest of granite and igneous rock that calls to walkers, mountain bikers and nature lovers alike. The 15km-long Malvern ridge, which divides the counties of Herefordshire and Worcestershire, is at such a dramatic elevation from the flat plains of the Severn Valley that from Worcestershire Beacon, its highest point, it is reputed that in the right conditions you can see 15 counties.

It was a fragile sun that cast its pale light on the eastern face of the Malvern range as I approached. Its pre-Cambrian bulk rises inexorably behind the town, and only as I neared the beginning of my ascent did I begin to appreciate its enormity, at least in relation to its surroundings, and the fact

---

INFO:

START/FINISH: Great Malvern station, Station Approach WR14 3AL, 52.108928, -2.318050

DISTANCE: 28.1 miles/45.2km   **ASCENT:** 5328ft/1624m   **OFF-ROAD:** 85%

TERRAIN: Narrow dirt track on the slopes; wider, smooth-flowing stony trails higher up. Most of the route is along the hills' steep slopes or the undulating ridgeline. The bridleway network to the north-west is flatter but muddier.

NAVIGATION: Straightforward. It's hard to go wrong on the Malverns themselves. There's such an array of trails along the spine of the hills it's better to make it up as you go along – you can't really get lost. Once you get to West Malvern, however, after Croft Bank you need to turn right into a farmyard before you'll see the bridleway sign, then keep right to take the path through a gate and into the woods. Make sure you turn left at the next junction of bridleways otherwise you'll find yourself on the return leg too soon. OS Landranger 149 and 150 are worth taking with you.

EAT AND DRINK:

The Red Lion, 4 St Ann's Road, Great Malvern, Worcestershire WR14 4RG, 01684 564787, www.redliongreatmalvern.co.uk

St Ann's Well Café, St Ann's Road, Great Malvern, Worcestershire WR14 4RF, 01684 560285, www.stannswell.co.uk

SLEEP:

Sydney House, 40 Worcester Road, Great Malvern, Worcestershire WR14 4AA, 01684 574994, www.sydneyhouse.co.uk

Out to Grass, Woodend Farm, Bromyard Road, Malvern, Herefordshire WR13 5JW, 01886 880099, www.outtograss.com

Bivvy: nr viewpoint at Worcestershire Beacon

PROVISIONS:

Crumpton Hill Farm Shop, Crumpton Hill Road, Malvern, Worcestershire WR13 5HP, 01886 880802

Back On Track Bikes, Unit 2, No 6 North Malvern Road, Malvern, Worcestershire WR14 4LT, 01684 565777, www.backontrack-bikes.com

that its surface is cross-crossed with some 160km of footpaths and bridleways. There's a two-tiered terrace of whitewashed shops and houses on its shallow foothills, behind which the barren beacon of North Hill, the second highest point on the Malverns at 397 metres, seemed to shake off its wooded shackles to keep watch over the town.

It was a struggle to heave the weight of my camping gear up these steep slopes. The earthy paths were moist and soft beneath the trees, but tended to drain well given the severity of the slopes. I usually savour every climb; settling into a rhythm and content to delay the gratification of the panorama that awaits on a hilltop. But I was keen to break through the treeline and take in the Malverns' magical views before the storm that I could feel as much as see brewing finally broke. I wasn't planning to reach North Hill until the next day; that afternoon I would ride south to explore most of the 20 named hills that run down the length of the Malverns' spine.

As I climbed I noticed a gradual transition in the vegetation through which the multitude of paths had been hewn. Oak and mountain ash trees gave way to sycamore and silver birch, and as I left a hollow path through a leafy plateau to make a final push for the top of Summer Hill, hawthorn turned to gorse, bramble and bracken, until that too receded as stony paths took me out into a clearing, the thin soil supporting little more than short wiry grasses and scrub.

From here I caught just a glimpse of the range of hills that unravelled to the south, but I'd come out too far down Summer Hill to find the expansive views I was looking for. Instead I'd arrived at Upper Wyche, the first of two cuttings through the hills, and ahead broiling clouds rolled across the southern hills. I could see far enough from here to watch as the sun's rays, like those of car headlamps, illuminated small patches of field in a darkening landscape, and I hurried on in a bid to clear this exposed stretch and find shelter on the lower slopes of the aptly named Perseverance Hill. Looking back the way I had come up to Worcestershire Beacon, which dominated the horizon, I could see how the Malverns had got their name – if indeed the word does come from the Celtic *moel bryn*, or 'bare hill' – and it was beneath these barren tops my route took me, until at last I reached my first summit, that of Black Hill.

The seething clouds only served to make a view that would be breathtaking in any condition, all the more dramatic. To the east shafts of light burst through purple clouds given a painterly flourish by the deluge they were unleashing upon the valley floor, while to the west Worcestershire's hills cascaded in ever-decreasing ripples from the feet of the Malverns. And remarkably I remained untouched by the storm, the hills seeming to have punctured a hole in the clouds.

I decided not to continue to the second cutting before Herefordshire Beacon, but instead about-turned and rode the crest of Pinnacle and Jubilee Hills, trying to commit these astounding views to memory, all the while scanning the

lower slopes for potential camp sites. Summer Hill defeated me and I was forced to dismount and push, taking another breather at the top and watching other riders flashing through the trees below me. From there it was a swooping track past sheep pens before another unforgiving climb, but I managed to stay aboard, intent on riding up to the county's pinnacle – that of Worcestershire Beacon. I ascended through wisps of cloud, slowly, painstakingly turning the pedals until I slumped at the foot of the ornate trig point.

While trying to catch my breath I noticed not only the other hill tops dwarfed below me, but a change in the light too. It had a strange, ethereal quality to it, yet also a startling clarity – augmented by the almost biblical battle raging in the early evening skies between light and darkness. Looking out to the west I realised I must be able to see Wales, while at the feet of these hills pinpricks of light from numerous villages and hamlets began to appear in the gloom.

I lingered a while, reluctant to leave this splendour behind but keen to seek shelter from a wholly uncertain sky, and suddenly noticed just yards beneath me a rocky crevice gouged into the slope.

Clambering down to investigate I discovered a cave-like shelter with enough of a grassy overhang to protect me from the elements. Despite the risk I couldn't turn down the chance to spend the night on the highest point for many miles around, to watch the sun set and rise on such an achingly beautiful scene. So it was here, in this naturally formed granite indentation just shy of the Malverns' 425-metre summit and overlooking what seemed to be the whole of Herefordshire, that I spread my bivvy, cooked up a supper fit for kings and soaked up the majesty of it all. Such satisfaction was tinged with trepidation, though, particularly as black clouds rolled in on the horizon. I zipped up my

jacket, pulled down my woollen hat and prepared for the storm's impact... but remarkably it never came. A few raindrops spattered my cheeks but the clouds, which had rumbled straight towards me at eye level, seemed to break up and dissipate on Summer Hill, before reforming to drench the Severn Valley once more.

The sun wrested free from the clouds just in time to shed its final fiery glow at my feet, and with that the prospect of being caught up here amid the deluge passed. As the evening lengthened I begin to hear sounds drifting up on the breeze to me from hundreds of metres below, and could pick out what sounded like a pub band coming from Great Malvern behind my encampment, and possibly a wedding reception somewhere out in the darkness before me. They were soon muffled by a breeze that buffetted my shelter throughout the night, but even that couldn't ruin this beautiful window on the world that I returned to, bleary eyed, in the early morning, and the knowledge that for a few hours at least I'd have the hills all to myself.

As I suspected it was not until I had crested North Hill and emerged from the chute of a tooth-loosening descent off End Hill that I encountered the first walkers of the day, and the hour was early enough to allow me to explore the meadows, woodlands and hidden bridlepaths of West Malvern and Old Storridge Common, before returning to the gentrified avenues of the old spa town. At St Ann's Well café, on the site of an 11th century hermitage, I looked up at the miniature figures climbing the slopes of North Hill, knowing that every one of them would be off the slopes before nightfall, and reflected on how rewarding it can be to defy convention sometimes, to do things a little differently from the norm, and take a risk once in a while. The rewards, on occasion, can be immeasurable.

RIDING ON THE EDGE

THE HIGH MOORS AND VALLEY FLOORS OF DERBYSHIRE'S DARK PEAK PROMISE A RIDE OF BEAUTIFUL CONTRASTS

I disembarked from the train out of Sheffield at Bamford, having already caught a glimpse of the kind of riding that awaited from the train window. The high moors looked bleak and unwelcoming in the fading light, and having seen some of the lyrical names bestowed upon the peaks and ridges in these parts – Black Tor, Foulstone Moor, even Madwoman's Stones – I was reminded of Tolkien's dark places

in Mordor. There's certainly something foreboding about these bleak tops, but I had been assured by an old friend who rode these peaks during his university days, and who would join me the next day to give me a guided tour of them, that the High Peaks offered some of the finest off-road riding in England.

I rode out along Ladybower reservoir to scout out a place to camp (my friend and I had talked

INFO:

START: Car park at Heatherdene S33 0BY, 53.370562, -1.697765 (or Bamford station, Station Approach S32 1EG, 53.339531, -1.689919)
FINISH: Edale station, Station Road S33 7ZN, 53.364876, -1.816596

DISTANCE: 19.7 miles/31.8km   **ASCENT:** 2857ft/871m   **OFF-ROAD:** 70% (although the reservoir road beyond the visitor centre is closed on weekends)

TERRAIN: Steep, rocky slopes, boggy moor tops, fireroads and quiet lanes. Severe climbs either side of a flat ride round the reservoir.

NAVIGATION: Tricky in the latter stages. Early on, when climbing to Whinstone Lee Tor go straight ahead; don't gain any more height toward Hurkling Stones – you'll soon see the descent to the reservoir. Apart from that, navigation around the water is straightforward. At Hope Cross, make sure you go straight ahead at a junction of five paths, to drop down to Jaggers Clough. If you find yourself climbing still here, or are able to see the reservoir once again, you'll need to retrace your steps. Use OS Landranger 110.

EAT AND DRINK:

Yorkshire Bridge Inn, Ashopton Road, Bamford, Derbyshire S33 0AZ, 01433 651361, www.yorkshire-bridge.co.uk

The Rambler Inn, Edale, Hope Valley, Derbyshire S33 7ZA, 01433 670268, www.theramblerinn.com

SLEEP:

Woodbine B&B, 18 Castleton Road, Hope, Derbyshire S33 6RD, 07778 113882, www.woodbine-hope.co.uk

Fieldhead Campsite, Edale, Hope Valley, Derbyshire S33 7ZA, 01433 670386, www.fieldhead-campsite.co.uk

Bivvy: by the southwest bank of Ladybower Reservoir

PROVISIONS:

Riverside Herb Centre, Cafe and Deli, Castleton Road, Hathersage, Derbyshire S32 1EG, 01433 651055

Peak District Cycle Hire, Fairholmes, Derwent, Bamford, Derbyshire S33 0AQ, 01433 651261, www.peakdistrict.gov.uk/cyclehire

briefly about meeting for a jar near the station until I was regaled with stories of the owner's tendency to brandish his shotgun if displeased by his patrons, and thought better of it). Walking over the dam at its southern end, I clambered up the banks to find shelter from the drizzle and a place from which to look out over the valley. The banks to the south-west were heavily wooded; the opposite side more sparsely so, the steep ridges thinning of vegetation as they stretched up to the tops of Bamford and Moscar Moors and Ladybower Tor. The villages of Ashopton and Derwent were intentionally flooded and 'drowned' during the construction of the reservoir before the Second World War, and while the former was demolished prior to flooding, much of Derwent village remained intact. The clock tower of the church remained visible above the water level until being demolished in 1947, and many other buildings rose above the surface like ghostly appari-tions during a dry summer a decade later.

My night was a fitful one, having struggled to find a flat surface on this steep embankment and to stay dry during an inclement evening. I warmed myself with a steaming mug of coffee as I noticed my friend riding over the dam to meet me. It was almost dark the evening before when I crossed the reservoir, and it was only that morning that I noticed two huge 'plugholes' – or so the locals call them. With a diameter of 24 metres, these stone bell-mouth overflows sit above the watermark, each sucking water into their gaping maws. No wild swimming here then, I thought, as we rode out over the Ladybower viaduct, then left the morning traffic behind to spin up a wide stony bridleway that twisted up to Highshaw Clough. There were 'cloughs' scattered all over the maps of the Dark Peaks I had studied before my arrival, and only then did I see how numerous these gorges and narrow ravines are,

no doubt caused by glacial movement gouging the landscape through the millennia.

Picking lines through the rocks and grinding up this unrelenting gradient had us gasping, even as we switched back on ourselves at what I remem-bered from my map reading to be another grisly named point – Cutthroat Bridge. The rewards were well worth our efforts though, as we levelled off three-quarters of the way up Whinstone Lee Tor for a panoramic view of the Y-shaped reservoir, the forest behind it, Lose Hill and Nether Moor casting their shadow over it all. It wasn't long before our now slender trail dropped off Derwent Edge, a hazardous descent that tested nerve and bike-handling skills in equal measure.

A squat stone shelter halfway down offered respite from the morning's last shower and an increasingly taxing trail. From here on down to the road along Ladybower's north-eastern tip the path was paved with regular stone setts, offering a steady though somewhat slippery descent to the valley floor. Down here our journey changed dramatically as we followed a flat fireroad north through the Upper Derwent Valley. We could have crossed at the dam that separated Ladybower and Derwent reservoirs but chose to continue north up to a third, Howden reservoir, where the gritstone crags didn't seem quite so immense. It was this dark, rough and hard sandstone – Millstone Grit – that coloured the entire landscape, in dry stone walls, houses and the craggy peaks, and gives the Dark Peak its name. Its southern cousin, the White Peak, is paler and feels less harsh somehow, due in most parts to its smoother limestone valleys.

It was a while before we encountered Millstone Grit again, as fireroads gave way to quiet lakeside roads that meandered along the water's edge and the forest fringes. The moors rose and fell in shallower arcs now, and we revelled in having

the road to ourselves, with cars banned from this stretch during weekends. We were also making the most of this easy-going tour of the reservoirs, knowing that harsh climbs awaited if we were to get out of the basin and down into the Hope Valley, and took a slight detour to the Fairholmes Visitor Centre and bike shop on the water's edge. Under brightening skies we devoured toasted paninis from the little booth that served as the café, and it became clear to me what a draw the Peaks are to those who love the outdoors. There were people of all ages milling about, taking a break from running, riding, climbing and walking these fascinating peaks and cloughs. I noted the soft burr of a Western Isles Scot as well as a Cornish drawl among the accents we overheard.

Running out of excuses to delay the inevitable, we tarried just a little longer, but the climbs kicked in long before we'd had time to digest lunch. It was wooded at first and manageable, yet we were still labouring as we passed the quizzical stares of forest school children up on Hagg Side. The next climb, however, defeated us. 'The Beast' as it is affectionately known by local riders is a notorious boulder-strewn descent where many a sandstone rock bears deep gouges caused by pedals and cranks as riders have tried to find the best line on their way down. It's no simple task pushing loaded bikes up its steep, twisting face, but it was certainly safer, though it took some time to push up to clearer, open pasture. The views though, were breathtaking; the tops, bathed in late afternoon sunshine, looked far from the foreboding moors we had glanced up at that morning, and grassy heath gradually gave way to dwarf shrubs punctuated by rocky outcrops. The sight of a mountain hare reinforced the impression that this is a truly wild place – though just over Nether Moor lies the railway line between Hope and Edale.

However, we weren't done with climbing. I was glad to tackle Jagger's Clough back in the saddle again, and where 'the Beast' had felt somewhat claustrophobic beneath the pines on a track cut by the timeless passage of water into the earth, here we greedily gulped lungfuls of cool air while the clough shallowed and an ever expanding vista unfurled. From here we identified High Neb and Whinstone Lee Tor behind us, and the hulking nebulous peak that dwarfed all others on the horizon could only be Kinder Scout, scene of the famous trespass of 1932 which became a precursor to the rights to roam that we now take for granted.

A movement out of the corner of my eye pulled my attention away from the slopes of Kinder Scout to the toy train pulling out of Hope station far below us. The bridle path that now rolled away before us took us further down the line to Edale, and a final freewheel with the wind in our faces took us to Clough Farm. The railway ran alongside us, though depressed into deep cuttings. Our progress to Edale was overshadowed by another peak, though at 476 metres Lose Hill would barely reach the shoulders of Kinder Scout, and as we rolled past the station to the perfectly placed pub nearby, the real 'beast' of the Dark Peaks rose up to its full height of 636 metres – the highest in the East Midlands, as if challenging us to tame it. And after our Ladybower loop (our horseshoe-shaped route had in real terms only covered the distance between two branch-line stations, Bamford and Edale) had given me a taste of what Dark Peak riding is all about, we agreed that next time we met that's exactly what we should set out to do.

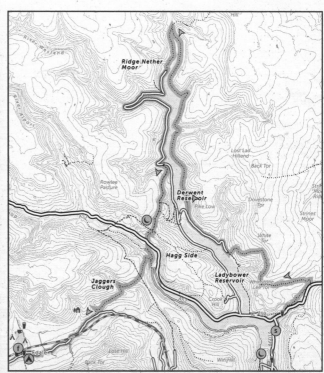

YORKSHIRE'S BLEAK BEAUTY

NEGOTIATING THE NORTH YORK MOORS' RIGGS, NABS AND DIALECT ALIKE MAKES FOR A MEMORABLE TRIP

The North York Moors rise out of the surrounding countryside, a peaty plateau that stretches to the North Sea. Deep valleys cut through the high moors and create huge fingers that reach out and suddenly drop away to the heather-smothered peat moors below, often coming to an abrupt halt at their tips – or 'nab' heads as they are known in these parts.

Heading east towards the North York Moors I was glad of the company of an old friend, who hails from Helmsley. The moors are a veritable playground for road riders and mountain bikers alike, with roadies flocking to tackle the one-in-four gradients of Sutton Bank, a staple climb in the

Tour of Britain over the years, while off-roaders head for Goathland, Danby, Fylingdales and Dalby Forest. For me, though, the beguiling yet bleak beauty of Rudland Rigg trumped all other choices, in part due to an unusual wild camping option that awaited us.

The two things that perhaps define the moors in general, and from my limited experience this area in particular, are the glorious purple heather, still flowering in September but turning more toward a burnt umber in colour, and the proliferation of game birds. I had never seen grouse and pheasant in such numbers as we rode north past the silent farmsteads of Rievaulx and Helmsley

---

INFO:

START/FINISH: Helmsley market place YO62 5BH, 54.246365, -1.061287

DISTANCE: 32.0 miles/51.5km   **ASCENT:** 3766ft/1148m   **OFF-ROAD:** 70%

TERRAIN: Boggy, peaty moorland, grassy tracks and stony bridleways. Flat moors can be heavy going and are regularly punctuated by tough dirt track climbs and gliding tarmac, or steep bridle path descents.

NAVIGATION: Difficult. You will need OS Landranger 100 throughout this ride. Take care along the bridlepaths below Beadlam Rigg, which can be very faint at times, and when approaching the rigg from Skiplam Moor stay close to the fenceline at the foot of the hill.

EAT AND DRINK:

Royal Oak Inn, Main St, Gillamoor, North Yorkshire YO62 7HX, 01751 431414, www.royaloakgillamoor.com

Lion Inn, Blakey Ridge, Kirkbymoorside, North Yorkshire YO62 7LQ, 01751 417320, www.lionblakey.co.uk

SLEEP:

YHA, Carlton Lane, Helmsley, North Yorkshire YO62 5HB, 0845 3719638, www.yha.org.uk

Bivvy: Rudland Rigg, 54.344745, -0.990207

PROVISIONS:

Hunters of Helmsley, 13 Market Place, Helmsley, North Yorkshire YO62 5BL, 01439 771307, www.huntersofhelmsley.com

Big Bear Bikes, Succours House, Southgate, Pickering, North Yorkshire YO18 8BL, 01751 474220, www.bigbearbikes.co.uk

Moors. They burst noisily from the grasses on all sides, warbling and clumsily taking wing, if only temporarily, and I could see what easy targets they must make for the shooting parties that flock here at weekends.

It's a singletrack road that runs out on to the moor, soon so remote as to be devoid of all traffic except the occasional farmer's Land Rover. By the time we left the road behind at Roppa Wood, a noticeable hush had descended, as well as a thick bank of fog, and for a while even the commotion of game birds scrabbling from beneath our wheels had ceased.

It had been a slow, steady ascent to the moor tops, and beneath the fog the landscape revealed itself at a similarly protracted rate. Back on a sliver of road that leads over Lund Ridge, the orange-tipped heather began to roll out invitingly to the east's horizon, with our ultimate destination, Rudland Rigg, rising unerringly in the distance, another 100 metres higher than our already lofty position. There aren't many villages or hamlets out on the moor, or much in the way of shelter, so we had planned our stops carefully. It pays to keep your bearings too, as many of the undesignated tracks up here tend to peter out in clumps of grasses and peat bogs and then reform soon after. It was these kinds of track we found ourselves on after the wider stony bridleway continued north, and we peeled off east, pushing our way up a punishing incline to Beadlam Rigg and unwittingly shepherding a worried flock of sheep off the slopes and into their enclosure.

From up here the views must be breathtaking; amid the gathering gloom they stayed hidden to us as thunder rolled overhead, and after gliding down a tarmac strip past golden bale-strewn fields we were glad of the shelter of Skiplam Wood as the storm broke. Here, a grassy bridleway turns on itself and plummets down a tight chute to a peaceful clearing through which one of the many streams or 'becks' on the moors flows.

Our rest stop, the inn at Gillamoor, was just a short climb away, up onto Boonhill Common, and it was here that I got a glimpse of one side of life on the North York Moors. The table outside the inn was cluttered with braces of pheasants, and inside a shooting party had gathered, fresh from their sport. Clutching pints of Black Sheep, they were clad in mossy tweeds and checks, an exclusive club of shoot organisers and their wealthy clients. I'm told that tens of thousands of pounds can often change hands for a weekend's shooting and hunting lodge hospitality, a fraction of which trickles down to the local farming community. And while the culture is so entrenched in the local way of life, to outsiders the breeding and wholesale slaughter of game birds can seem brutal and barbaric.

However, this centuries-old practice does have an unexpected benefit for wild campers hardy enough to spend a night out on the moor tops. Our journey soon took us out onto Rudland Rigg, up another gradual slope where tarmac receded and reddish sandy soil took over and carpeted our way to the uppermost part of the rigg. Off the main track near its 370 metre peak we had to dismount and pick our way through the heavy peat bog. But it was here, as it was for the shooting party in Gillamoor, that our quarry awaited. Every 20 metres or so lies a moss and heather covered shooting shelter, open to the sky but walled and dug into the heather, with a welcoming dry gravel floor. We found one that was just a little longer than most, and just enough off the top to be out of the worst of the wind, and in the dwindling light we set about making camp. Our tarp pegs sank nicely into the turf tops of the wall, leaving

a window on the world to the east that, given the clear skies that evening, promised to give us an unobstructed view of a beautiful sunrise the next morning. The sun's last rays illuminated Blakey Ridge before us as we sipped a much-need brew; it had grown noticeably colder but our bunker was more comfortable than we could have hoped for. Our final treat was a stellar show that grew more intense as the ambient light diminished. With such little light pollution here (Kirbymoorside to the south is all that gives the horizon a faint glow), the stars were crystal clear and I had to thank the shoot organisers for their unwitting and mercifully free hospitality; for me their hunting lodges could not have afforded such priceless views.

Our promised sunrise didn't disappoint and we were already awake as its early reddish glow crept in through our window. I was disappointed to leave our perfect camp, knowing it was particular to this place, but a decent night's sleep had set us up for our final leg back to Helmsley, which promised to be far from flat. Pushing our laden bikes back onto the rigg, we enjoyed the luxury of a freewheeling descent to start the morning. We were dropping down into Sleightholme Dale, losing much of yesterday's hard-won height, but what a way to lose it – the wide track that skirts sheep enclosures on Rudland Slack was reduced to a technical stony singletrack descent that swooped down over another bubbling beck into dappled woodland shade, before widening and rising once more, sweeping out of the trees and disintegrating into sporadic traces across the peaty grassland.

We picked our lines carefully, losing them along this sliver of a trail before purposefully abandoning it at the foot of the nab to Beadlam Rigg, the crossing point in our figure-of-eight ride. We didn't want to retrace our route or climb unnecessarily to the rigg, so we hugged the fence-line beneath its slopes and past the nab, focusing on a small stone farmstead that marked a return to discernible tracks, if also to climbing. But this time it was shallow and not to full ridge-height; just enough to ensure not another pedal stroke was needed once we reached the brow. It was a descent to savour, an opportunity to take in the moors' vast and colourful expanse, before opting for a wooded bridleway crossing of Riccal River to avoid Helmsley's main road and a final tarmac straight, past Carlton's church tower and back into the market town's bustling square.

We exchanged knowing smiles as we came to rest outside the town's country-wear outfitters, as we wondered how many of yesterday's customers in Gillamoor's Inn were also regulars here. I wondered where I had seen the name of this outfitters before, until my friend pointed out its name had been emblazoned across every disused cartridge we'd picked out of the bunker before making our beds last night. Still, there is one thing I have in common with this exclusive Yorkshire set, I had discovered – a shared love of local Black Sheep ale. And having shared my journey across the moors with a one-time local lad, I'd chosen the right company for picking the perfect post-ride pub too.

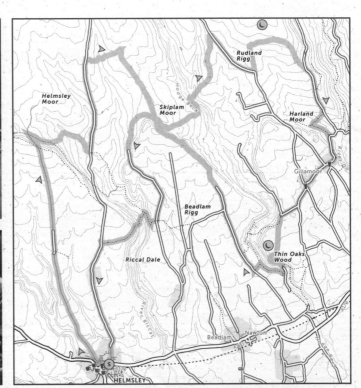

HIGH HILLS, DEEP DALES

AN EXPLORATION OF THE GLORIOUS YORKSHIRE DALES PROMISES TO BE A RIDE ON THE WILD SIDE

There are only 80 kilometres between the Yorkshire Moors and Dales yet they display distinct geological idiosyncrasies. While both enjoy the protection of National Park status and are scattered with characterful stone villages, that is where the similarities end. Whereas the moors are swathed in peat bog and purple heather, and their slopes fewer and steeper, the Yorkshire Dales are characterised by a patchwork of verdant, sloping, grazing pasture, divided by a haphazard grid of dry stone walls. The hills here are more undulating, rising westwards from the Vale of York and stretching across the Pennines, their valleys draining eastwards into the Ouse and the Humber, and apart from the valley villages, flat trails are in short supply.

So where to ride in the Dales? Malhamdale, Ribblesdale, Wensleydale, Nidderdale? If it has a 'dale' in its name, there's sure to be great off-road riding to be found. Pen-y-ghent, notably dale-less, has as much of an epic, isolated feel to a ride as any you'll find in the Dales, but I headed to Swaledale, on the eastern fringe of the National Park, often described as the best ride in the best dale. Dissected by the River Swale, my route would rise north out of the valley at Fremington, sweep over Reeth Low Moor before plunging back down to the river only to climb again to explore Whiteside, Harkerside and East Bolton moors, and eventually returning to the river at Grinton and Fremington. Along its 37km length lay some 1,300m of climbing; apart from a

---

INFO:

START/FINISH: Dales Bike Centre, Fremington DL11 6AW, 54.386055, -1.930614

DISTANCE: 23.1miles/37.1km   **ASCENT:** 4320ft/1317m   **OFF-ROAD:** 80%

TERRAIN: Mostly wide stony or grassy tracks, occasional boggy peat paths; constant undulations with a little respite along the Swale.

NAVIGATION: Difficult throughout. Use OS Landranger 98 or Explorer OL30; the latter is particularly helpful for negotiating Whitaside Moor and Reeth Low Moor.

EAT AND DRINK:

Overton House Café, Reeth, Richmond, North Yorkshire DL11 6SY, 01748 884045, www.overtonhousecafe.com

Bridge Inn, Grinton, Richmond, North Yorkshire DL11 6HH, 01748 884224, www.bridgeinn-grinton.co.uk

SLEEP:

Grinton Lodge YHA, Grinton, Richmond, North Yorkshire DL11 6HS, 0845 371 9636, www.yha.org.uk

Bivvy: Horse Pasture Wood

PROVISIONS:

Reeth Bakery, Silver Street, Reeth, Richmond, North Yorkshire DL11 6SP, 01748 884735

Dales Bike Centre, Parks Barn, Fremington, Richmond, North Yorkshire DL11 6AW, 01748 884908, www.dalesbikecentre.co.uk

road stretch out of Healaugh, it promised to be 'up hill and down dale' all the way.

Given how wild and exposed this ride would feel at times, starting it from the Dales Bike Centre in Fremington gave this loop a reassuring trail-centre feel. With a café, bunkhouse, bike wash and free parking, it's the perfect place from which to explore this achingly beautiful corner of the Dales. As I set out along NCN route 71, my flirtation with a waymarked road route was a brief one, as I knew it would be. Whereas the NCN route meanders through the Arkengarthdale valley, and beckoned the roadies who shared my departure from Fremington, my route lured me ever closer to the daunting escarpment of Fremington Edge. When sketching out my route I noted with concern that the contours that marked the Edge on my OS map were so close, it looked like the entire face of the slope had been coloured in orange felt tip. However I also noticed a bridleway that left the climb early to traverse the face around a third of the way up. I'd see how I felt on the day, I'd thought then.

Now, with my bike under load, it was already a strain as I followed the 'High Fremington' sign away from Reeth to tackle the Edge. At first the road rose at a shallow gradient, and soon my bail-out bridleway had come and gone; I couldn't take the easy way out so soon into a ride. Yet in true Dales fashion the road quickly gave up the ghost, fading to a mere track that got rockier as it got steeper. It was now a granny ring grind, but a distraction from the early toil was the view that began to open up behind me as I climbed – a bucolic vision of pale stone villages and hamlets clustered along the banks of the Swale and Arkle Beck below me. All else was hulking promontories that looked as if they were wrapped in green baize and criss-crossed with silver thread, as the sun caught the myriad stone boundary walls. Only ahead of me did the diorama take on a greyer, less vibrant hue; though the old quarry workings atop Hurst Moor would offer some respite from the technical, rocky ascent that had already defeated me.

Pushing to the top of the Edge left me some 450 metres above sea level – as high as I'd reach all day – and after pausing to take in the complete view my efforts afforded me, it was time to reap another reward. After picking my way through the quarry detritus, the trail dropped off the Edge, becoming grassier and less technical but no less enjoyable as it ran alongside the fantastically named hamlet of Booze, into Arkle Town. Down here the road riders were cutting their teeth on the Long Causeway climb, which would soon ferry them freewheeling down to Reeth, but once again my trail was a solitary one, apart from the occasional horse or hardy rambler as I crossed the road onto a reassuringly solid stone track across peaty moorland. It was a lovely gradual climb, which cut between Calver and Cringley Hill and soon presented me with another fine valley view, albeit under broiling black cloud cover, this time down to Feetham and Healaugh.

As the trail became fainter and boggier it crossed a promising white ribbon of stony single-track that ran away east straight down to Reeth; instead I opted for a long grassy descent over gradually firming ground, bumping and tossing me around in the saddle for some 3km back down to the Swale. I was hoping to make it to Healaugh before the storm clouds above me released their payload, but the rain hit me full in the face before I was halfway down. By the time I reached the sleepy hamlet I was drenched, and with no pub or café in sight I made do with a telephone box to shelter me, as thunder rumbled beyond the moors. As telephone boxes go it was surprisingly plush, boasting a carpet, waste bin and fresh flowers, but the realisation soon dawned that this wasn't a passing shower and the evening was almost upon me. I had planned to camp out on the edge of Horse Pasture Wood, a neat square of deciduous woodland on the south bank of the Swale, over-looking the bridge halfway between Feetham and Healaugh, but I decided to cut my losses and bolted back to the bunkhouse in Fremington. I could ride straight through Reeth along the road but I was already soaked and with the promise of a hot shower beckoning I rode down to the stone bridge over the Swale at Low Whita and took a bridleway that hugged the river bank past my intended camp for the night (now looking decidedly dank and chill, though it would have been a lovely spot to camp were I not already drenched, and with some prospect of an end to the deluge).

There's no shame in bailing out of a wild camp in such circumstances, I told myself, having showered and changed, as I headed down to the inn at Grinton, just a few hundred metres from the bike centre, in search of a hot supper. It may still have been lashing it down outside, but the next day was set to be fair, so I headed back to the warmth of the bunkhouse hopeful of a memorable end to my tour of these dales.

Back at the bridge in the morning my spirits were much higher than last night's brief encounter. The clouds were low and sullen, but at least the rain had passed. The rolling road out of Low Lane ushered me up towards another mirth-inducing village name – this time Crackpot – before veering off up the slopes of High Lane towards the promise of more moorland trails over Whiteside Moor. It had a much wilder feeling to it here than the pasture-covered slopes to the north of the river, and I could see how the moor got its name, with a barren swathe of white stone and slate keeping the grass at bay.

Another old mine lies forgotten up here, one remnant of which came into view as I rattled along a rocky path past a deep gulley. I dropped down to the valley floor, which under the low cloud cover felt particularly dark and hushed. A stony track soon yielded to softer ground as I climbed to the cairned summit, then as the mine workings receded a final bridleway then road descent carried me through familiar lush pasture and over the wide banks of the Swale at Grinton and into Fremington once more. Over a coffee and running repairs in the bike centre's workshop, I rested my aching legs and reflected on the unforgiving nature of these hills, and how for me that somehow increases their appeal. A ride like the one I had just completed leaves you feeling that you've taken on nature's wilder reaches, and even if the elements do their damnedest to drive you away, exposing yourself to them gives you a taste of what wild riding is all about, and you can't help being left wanting more. This may have been my first visit to the Yorkshire Dales, but I promised myself it wouldn't be my last.

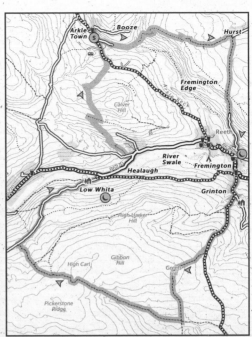

RISING TO THE CHALLENGE

THE HIGH PASSES BETWEEN BUTTERMERE AND ENNERDALE PROVIDE AS STIFF A TEST AS ANY ADVENTURE RIDE CAN MUSTER - AND EVEN GREATER REWARDS

Buttermere heralded an entirely different Lake District experience to my Grizedale Forest adventure (ride no.23). Whereas the shores of Lake Windermere are wooded and shielded from breezes off the lake or the unpredictable Cumbrian weather, the Buttermere Valley is exposed and feels much more isolated. There weren't nearby towns such as Ambleside to retreat to should the weather turn or I needed provisions, and the hills aren't so much a picturesque backdrop as towering over you. No, this was a microadventure that promised to be of macro proportions, through Gale Fell and Banna Fell to Croasdale then along the shores of Ennerdale Water to traverse the Scarth Gap Pass beneath the shadow of Hay Stacks. An arduous, barren and exposed journey awaited, and I needed to make particular preparations for it.

How incongruous then that Buttermere itself is a pleasant village set in the heart of a lush valley – quite a contrast to the barren, lunar-like terrain you'll encounter if approaching from the south-east. Despite the rugged hills, the valleys here are verdant and fertile in places. Indeed it is likely that Buttermere derives from Old English and means 'lake by the dairy

INFO:

START/FINISH: Car park, Buttermere, CA13 9UZ, 54.540696, -3.277531

DISTANCE: 17.4 miles/28.0km   **ASCENT:** 3011ft/918m   **OFF-ROAD:** 90%

TERRAIN: A mix of wide, stony lakeside trails and challenging hillside tracks, which are boggy, stony and highly technical. Two arduous climbs and tricky descents are punctuated by flat lakeside paths.

NAVIGATION: Difficult through the high passes. The bridleways along Buttermere, Crummock Water and Ennerdale Water are well signed, as are the turnings up through Gale Fell and Scarth Gap Pass. However don't veer left up Scale Beck or right up Mosedale on the way through Gale Fell; GPS support will make sure you stay on track through both passes.

EAT AND DRINK:

The Fish Inn, Buttermere, Cumbria CX13 9XA, 01768 770253, www.fishinnbuttermere.co.uk

The Fox & Hounds, Ennerdale Bridge, Cumbria CA23 3AR, 01946 861373, www.foxandhoundsinn.org

SLEEP:

The Bridge Hotel, Buttermere, Cumbria CX13 9UZ, 01768 770252, www.bridge-hotel.com

Syke Farm Campsite, Buttermere Village, Cumbria CA13 9XA, 01768 770222

Bivvy: Bowness Knott, Ennerdale Water

PROVISIONS:

Croft House Farm Cafe, Buttermere, Cumbria CA13 9XA, 01768 770235, www.crofthousefarmcafe.co.uk

Whinlatter Bikes, 82 Main Street, Keswick, Cumbria CA12 5DX, 01768 773940, www.whinlatterbikes.com

pastures' (another theory is that it once belonged to an 11th century chieftain named Buthar and became known as 'Buthar's mere').

Having spoken to local riders and discovered there would be unrideable sections along the transitions between Buttermere and Ennerdale, I stripped back my bike and kit to the bare essentials, making it easier to shoulder when needed. My tent and sleeping bag were swapped for micro-light versions, the frame bag dispensed with, and lighter rigid carbon forks and lower gearing installed on the bike.

However as I passed Wilkinsyke Farm's pleasant pasture between Buttermere Lake and its nearby twin Crummock Water I felt my preparations and precautions had been excessive. The trail out of the National Trust village was wide, flat and firm, though strewn with puddles that reflected a low monochrome sky. Recent rain didn't bode well for my ascent through Scale Knott, where the bridleway would hug the saturated banks of Scale Beck. I was more concerned about my return journey through Scarth Gap Pass, primarily because I could find no-one who had ridden it, but also because its gradients looked steep and the whole face of High Crag and the forebodingly named Sheepbone Buttress were riddled with becks and falls. The scree-scattered descent promised to be as treacherous as the climb.

Still, I tried to banish all thoughts of what may be to come; after all my descent towards Gatesgarth wouldn't be until the following day. I was hoping to find a sheltered spot along the banks of Ennerdale, undoubtedly a more hospitable place than these high, hostile-looking hills. Despite, or maybe because of, the sheer scale of my surroundings I felt almost hemmed in. With Whiteless Pike, Knott Rigg and Hindscarth behind me – the latter towering to 727 metres high – and my no less formidable quarry ahead, my only real respite was the tranquil lake shores. However, the gentle rhythm of Crummock

Water lapping on the shore, at times only a few metres from the trail, was soon left behind. Already I could see Scale Beck cascading down off the lower slopes of Scale Knott, and knew my path would for a time run alongside it.

The trail was easy to make out at first, so trampled had it become by the many walkers who venture tentatively away from the lake-side paths, but soon the slopes rose, the scree abounded and the scrubland became so saturated as to deter all but the hardiest of walkers. Still I was heartened to see faint wheel tracks ahead, so presumed the trail would not become impenetrable, and pressed on. Though soon mere traces, the tracks disappeared into saturated scrub and between clusters of jagged stone, only to reappear further on. By the time I had reached the upper reaches of Scale Beck, the quagmire had dissolved all traces of human traffic, and I began to despair that I would have to resort not only to hike-a-bike but also to constantly studying the GPS to make sure I was on track.

Along the raised valley floor between Gale Fell, Hen Combe and Mosedale I was able to remount, and was pleased to be able to study my surroundings a little, while I was no longer glued to my screen. The path wound its way along an almost triangular plain, the protected slopes a warmer, richer hue than the harsh crags of Hay Stacks and their surroundings, which I had passed on my way into Buttermere through Gatesgarth.

The respite was welcome, though brief. Next up was the climb to Floutern Tarn below Whiteoak Moss. I managed to stay mounted thanks to my modified gear ratio, but at times it was excruciating, and I ground my way up a 150 metre technical climb in a little over a kilometre. The wind was whipping ripples across the tarn as I passed, and my descent down to the road near the hamlet of Croasdale was in the face of squally showers and buffeting wind. It made an

already demanding descent even more taxing, and by the end I was gingerly picking my way between rough slabs of wet rock at a pedestrian pace.

Once on tarmac I decided to make an unscheduled stop at nearby Ennerdale Bridge, where the warmth of its pub proved a welcome way to sit out the showers. My bedraggled appearance prompted some banter at the bar, where one of the locals looked alarmed when I told him I was planning to ride through Scarth Gap Pass tomorrow. "You'd be quicker walking", he informed me, and it was with his comment in mind that I left somewhat despondently once the wind and rain had died down.

I set out along Ennerdale's northern shore at dusk, the track becoming increasingly saturated towards the aptly-named Mireside, I noted with a rueful smile. Still, the glimpse of a setting sun lightened my mood and lent a warm tinge to the clouds if not my limbs. I decided to camp on higher, sheltered ground given the inclement weather, and noticed the high mound of Bowness Knott protruding from the tips of the pines at the western fringe of Ennerdale Forest. From the clearing I enjoyed not only the forest's protection but also fine views over the lake, framed by the ridges of the high fells beyond.

I had envisioned camping on the shores, enjoying a leisurely supper by the fire. In truth it was more of a perfunctory experience; the dead wood was too wet for a fire, the air too chill to sit out for long, so with all my layers still on I zipped up the tent and my bag and got my head down for the night. My immediate thoughts on waking were of the pass I had to tackle, which during the night seemed to have taken on epic, almost mythical proportions. I banished these thoughts over a breakfast of porridge and nuts and headed back out to rejoin my trail. I soon realised I was dawdling, clearly making the most of a pleasant path between the treeline and lake. As the lake soon receded, in

a gap in the trees I could make out the stony crag of Red Pike looming high above the trees. It served to shake me out of my reverie and steel my resolve.

As I rode alongside the River Liza I could just about make out the path that runs precariously between the peaks of High Stile and High Crag, knowing I would soon be joining it. I craned my neck to see the scree-covered slopes of High Crag tumble down into the pass, and my heart was almost in my mouth as I doubled back on a bridle path that rose away from the river and rapidly disintegrated as I left the trees' embrace and began to scale the grey slopes. The pass seemed to start out as it meant to go on, pitching immediately up and weaving between huge slabs of rock that had gathered over millennia at the feet of these two giants – Hay Stacks and High Crag. It was just as I had feared, an insurmountable mixture of blunt boulders, boggy scrub and jagged scree, over all of which ran a network of ice-cold rivulets, like me trying to find the path of least resistance. I managed to ride much further than I expected, though, albeit at a laughably low cadence, before succumbing to the unrelenting gradient and lack of traction. I was heartened when I saw Hay Stacks was already behind me by the time I finally dismounted, walking a weary kilometre and eventually shouldering the bike up a staggering one-in-four segment. The pass finally peaked at 450 metres, but the descent was no less challenging. In parts I still had to push, but for most of the 2km drop to lake-level I stayed mounted, using every last ounce of energy and testing my handling skills to the limit. Never before, I realised as I rumbled over Peggy's Bridge and hit reassuringly firm ground through Burtness Woods, had I exhausted myself so utterly going down-hill.

Back at Buttermere I slumped over my bars taking laboured breaths. Then I noticed it: beneath the tiredness, the burning in my thighs and the aching in my wrists, there was another feeling, and one that I hadn't expected. I could only describe it as exhilaration.

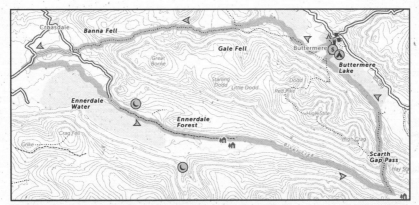

TAMING THE WILDS
OF WINDERMERE

THIS SHORT SCENIC LAKE DISTRICT LOOP BETWEEN GRIZEDALE AND WINDERMERE IS AN IDEAL INTRODUCTION TO BIKEPACKING FOR YOUNGSTERS

The Lake District boasts some of the finest mountain bike trails anywhere in the British Isles. I've ridden Helvellyn and Skiddaw in the past, two of England's highest peaks, and they proved as stern a test of skill and stamina as I have encountered on two wheels. Yet as well as the likes of Helvellyn and Borrowdale in the north of the Lakes, some wonderful family-friendly trails can be found further south in Grizedale Forest, where an array of natural and waymarked routes draw mountain bikers of all ages in droves.

That's not to say the southern lakes are bereft of challenging trails. Rock gardens, jagged descents and technical climbs abound, while the mountain passes of Walna Scar and Nan Bield take some beating in terms of a sense of true wilderness. We left such immense silhouettes lingering enticingly in the distance, though, as it was to Grizedale I had brought my sons to give them a taste of bikepacking adventures, though I hoped the distant mountains would give them a tantalising glimpse of how far, how high and how wild a mountain bike can take

INFO:

START/FINISH: Hawkshead car park, LA22 0NB, 54.373830, -2.996045

DISTANCE: 13.8 miles/22.2km   **ASCENT:** 2283ft/696m   **OFF-ROAD:** 85%

TERRAIN: Rolling forest trails, paved doubletrack and muddy lake-side trails. There are two fast descents but after leaving Hawkshead most of the climbing is done gradually.

NAVIGATION: Straightforward. The trail is waymarked on the edge of Grizedale forest, and the bridle paths are well signposted. Stay close to the shore all the way along Windermere up to Wray Castle. In the woods at Long Height five paths intersect; make sure you take the furthest right and continue straight ahead down into Colthouse. OS Landrangers 90 and 97 are useful for exploring the area.

EAT AND DRINK:

Tower Bank Arms, Near Sawrey, Ambleside, Cumbria LA22 0LF, 015394 36334, www.towerbankarms.co.uk

Cuckoo Brow Inn, Far Sawrey, Ambleside, Cumbria LA22 0LQ, 015394 43425, www.cuckoobrow.co.uk

SLEEP:

Low Wray campsite, Low Wray, Ambleside, Cumbria LA22 0JA, 015394 63862, www.nationaltrust.org.uk

Bivvy: Belt Ash Coppice

PROVISIONS:

Sun Cottage Tea Rooms, Main Street, Hawkshead, Ambleside, Cumbria LA22 0NT, 015394 36123

Velo Bikes, Grizedale Visitor Centre, Hawkshead, Ambleside, Cumbria LA22 0QJ, 01229 860369

you, without defeating them or deflating their enthusiasm. I didn't want us to join the procession of riders cruising along the waymarked Forestry Commission routes that radiate from the trail centre; instead our route ran along mostly natural trails.

As it was late October I treated us to a touch of 'glamping' at the National Trust campsite at Low Wray on the banks of Lake Windermere. That way I knew we wouldn't be over-burdened on our ride and would have decent protection from the notoriously fickle Cumbrian weather. It may have been far removed from the wild camping ethos at the heart of bikepacking, but I didn't want to put the boys off with a cold, uncomfortable night under a tarp.

Along the banks of Esthwaite Water every other car we passed seemed to be laden with bikes. Grizedale's all-weather forest trails still seemed to be pulling in the crowds late in the year, and sure enough they were all heading towards the trail centre. We, however, parked up just past the water's northern shore, where Black Beck flows through the heart of the village. I was almost reluctant to head south-west to the cycle trails of Hawkshead Moor, anxious that the boys would rather mess around among the crowds of recreational cyclists riding their leisurely loops, but they seemed excited by the prospect of going 'off-grid' and barely noticed that we'd soon left the teeming forest paths behind. It was a steady climb out of Hawkshead, along leafy lanes then muddy bridle paths, but soon we were swinging east before getting too close to the bustling outdoor activities centre at Grizedale and dropping down a slippery trail towards the southern shores of Esthwaite Water.

Even the narrow village lanes were busy with traffic, but our route barely touched the tarmac. A brief melee aside at Near Sawrey, another lovely little lake-side village, we stuck to peaceful trails enjoying the quiet, save for light-hearted conversation and the crunch of our wheels through a mat of fallen leaves. The trees and hedgerows had a rich, deep autumnal hue, a welcome warm glow to the landscape on that chill afternoon. We hadn't gone far but I was keen not to tax the lads too much, so we stopped at Far Sawrey's busy pub for hot brews before tackling the muddy climb that led us half-way up the 18km-long shoreline of Windermere, England's largest natural lake.

Skirting from one lake shore to another, I had presumed the ride would be fairly flat but riding through woods with names like Penny Brow Wood and Tanner Brow I shouldn't have been surprised by the undulation between shorelines. We left the wide lanes outside Far Sawrey behind a washed-out sun struggling to penetrate the canopy of Cuckoo Brow Wood. By the time we hurtled down the slippery banks of Barrow Slack it had given up the ghost entirely. It was a steep slope down to the water's edge, and for the boys it was a mirth-inducing descent, locking brakes and skidding down the leafy slope to pull up just short of Windermere's lapping shore. Past Belle Isle, an island that almost straddles the lake across its width, a ferry made its way over to Bowness, but the mist and gloom seemed to soften the sound of its engine and apart from that it was a silent, beguiling scene.

From here on, after some obligatory stone skimming, it was a fantastic lake-side ride all the way up to Low Wray on a firm and easy-going track. The boys were enjoying themselves more than I could have hoped, and raced ahead eager to find the campsite. We emerged from the wooded banks at Belle Grange only to disappear back into the trees as the track became metalled and turned inland while we continued to hug the waterline, this time along saturated singletrack. The boys' wheels were sending up a fountain of water so I hung back eager to avoid an early shower. Unsurprisingly we were all spattered with mud by the time we arrived at Wray

Castle, having spotted its prominent turrets way back at Balla Wray. It's a wonderful Victorian neo-Gothic building now under the auspices of the National Trust and was in its element then, at Halloween, with each cobweb-draped window illuminated by a flickering pumpkin lantern and even a headless doorman greeting visitors at the main entrance.

It was dusk by the time I persuaded the boys to leave, so it was by lamplight that we rode in procession into Low Wray. Our berber tent, much like a yurt, was deep in the woods, and the entire site had a pleasingly natural feel to it. As we rode up the path we passed occasional wooden camping pods and the odd tarp-and-hammock arrangement, and though quiet and densely wooded, all notions of wild camping were dispelled when we rolled up to the tent's split saloon-type wooden door. Inside, illuminated by fairy lights, were a double bed and two futons, as well a dining table, kitchenette with a two-ring gas-fired burner and – the piece de resistance – a wood-burning stove in the centre of the tent, with its flue extruding through the middle of the tent's pointed roof.

It was unashamed glamping, but the boys loved it and set about getting a fire started. I retreated outside to build one of my own, on stones foraged from the woods, and the boys didn't need much persuading to join me round our al fresco fire for an evening barbeque. Within minutes they'd hauled every duvet and blanket out from the tent, and sat chatting contentedly by the fire. After supper, when they'd retreated to the warmth of the tent and the one proper bed, I sat outside a while longer and wondered if they would be ready for a wilder trip.

After a morning of exploring our surroundings and canoeing along inlets that snaked through the campsite we set off by road, back south to High Wray before climbing slowly to Long Height and plunging deep into Fleming Wood, skirting the ancient earthwork of Latterbarrow which protruded high above the treeline.

The forest trail twisted languidly west, cutting between still ponds then across a clearing before dropping, off-camber down a grassy bank to Colthouse. Needless to say the boys were whooping and hollering as they barrelled down the slope, once again clearly enjoying the ride. Colthouse and Town End were no more than a smattering of dwellings at the outskirts of Hawkshead, and we emerged onto a quiet lane that led us back over Black Beck where we began our little adventure the day before.

On the way home it was too soon for me to introduce the idea of throwing wild camping into the mix, but soon the boys were asking me how I spend my nights on my 'grown-up' adventure rides. When I explained why I use a bivvy, and that sometimes I don't even bother with a tarp for shelter, there was silence. I've scared them off, I thought, somewhat crestfallen. Then my eight-year-old piped up and said, 'Dad, can you buy us a bivvy?' That seed is beginning to take root, by the looks of things.

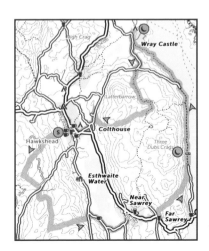

SCOTLAND & WALES

A ROOM WITH A VIEW

ADVENTURE BIKING DOESN'T GET MUCH WILDER THAT THIS ISLE OF MULL EPIC FROM TOBERMORY TO THE REMOTE TOMSLEIBHE BOTHY

Hailing from the Western Isles, my father had often spoken of the beguiling beauty of the Isle of Mull, and having discovered there was a particularly remote bothy on the Glenforsa estate, I came to discover the place for myself. I started from the ferry port of Craignure and my journey to Tomsleibhe bothy took me from the colourful capital Tobermory, around the northern peninsula in search of views of the Isle of Coll, through the forests of Glen Gorm and Glen Aros and up the Glenforsa estate to the isolated bothy deep in the heart of the mountains.

There are some wonderful additional trails close to the 480km of coastline, but you are never far from the sea on this route, and as I soon discovered, the island's spellbinding beauty can be felt wherever you go on Mull. For me, this journey was about reaching one of the most remote bothies in Scotland and discovering what true wilderness means on an island where on average only three people live per square kilometre. During the Highland clearances of the 18th and 19th centuries, the isle's population fell from 10,000 to 3,000, from which the figure has barely

INFO:

START: Tobermory harbour, PA75 6PR, 56.623581, -6.062506
FINISH: Tomsleibhe bothy, PA65 6BA, 56.466681, -5.869218

DISTANCE: 30 miles/40.2km (43.3 miles/61.5km returning via glen path and A649 to Craignure ferry terminal)
ASCENT: 2194ft/669m   **OFF-ROAD:** 80% (60% with Craignure extension)

TERRAIN: Forest paths, firm doubletrack and fireroads through the glen. A sharp climb out of Tobermory and fast descent into Salen then flat through the glen until the final ramp to the bothy.

NAVIGATION: Fairly easy. Look out for the forest trail on the right at the treeline as you leave Tobermory; the track south from Glengorm castle is also unsigned. The Glenforsa estate is well signposted, though you'll need to go through a gate marked 'no entry' to get to the bothy, to which access is permitted. Don't cross the Forsa river by the footbridge, but use the stepping stones 1,500m further up the path. OS Landrangers 47 and 49 would be useful.

EAT AND DRINK:

The Mishnish, Main Street, Tobermory, Isle of Mull, Argyll PA75 6NT, 01688 302500, www.themishnish.co.uk

The Bellachroy, Dervaig, Isle of Mull, Argyll PA75 6QW, 01688 400314, www.thebellachroy.co.uk

SLEEP:

Dervaig Hostel, Dervaig Village Hall, Dervaig, Isle of Mull, Argyll PA75 6QN, 01688 400491, www.mull-hostel-dervaig.co.uk

Tobermory Campsite, Newdale Cottage, Dervaig Road, Tobermory, Isle of Mull, Argyll PA75 6QF, 01688 302624, www.tobermory-campsite.co.uk

Tomsleibhe bothy, 56.466681, -5.869218

PROVISIONS:

Tobermory Bakery and Coffee Shop, Main Street, Tobermory, Isle of Mull, Argyll PA75 6NU

Browns (for bike parts and hire), 21 Main Street, Tobermory, Isle of Mull, Argyll PA75 6NX, 01688 302020, www.brownstobermory.co.uk

deviated since. Less than a century ago, in fact, there were more sheep than people on the island.

As I arrived in Tobermory I remembered tales of a galleon from the defeated Spanish Armada sinking in the bay, reputedly laden with gold bullion, as well as more recent (and probably more accurate) accounts of minke whales spotted off the Sound. Though scarce, golden eagles are more commonly found here than anywhere else in the UK and many visitors to Mull come here with the express purpose of spotting them.

Tobermory is situated on a small rounded headland at the northern tip of the Sound of Mull, but is banked by dense deciduous forest, through which my route took me north-west, away from the gaudily daubed houses of Tobermory Bay and into a world of emerald green, muted olives and burnt umber. A firm track cut through the woods, leading me past waterfalls where sea cliffs dropped away into Ardmore Bay. I neared the fairytale-esque Glengorm Castle, with princely B&B rooms in its towers, before the trail doubled back and the trees yielded to barren scrub along exposed, undulating slopes until the wooded banks of Loch Frisa.

Away from the coastal winds it was unnervingly silent through Salen Forest and Glen Aros, save for the crunch of my tyres along the wide, dry loch-side trails that didn't even appear on my dad's decade-old map. It was something of a shock to be confronted by traffic an hour later as the trail dropped and the forest ended abruptly at the Salen road. The mainland was hidden behind a veil of fog, as I rode along the bay at Salen, and as I passed an old coastal landing strip I wondered if I should have stopped in the village, but with no idea how rough the 6km Glenforsa estate trail would be and with maybe 90 minutes of daylight left, I pressed on. I had all the food I needed for my bothy night and the prospect of groping my way along what my OS map suggested

was a wild, barren and remote glen in fading twilight in search of a mountain bothy was not one I relished. Yet my dad's Landranger also showed a fairly flat and straight trail that ran alongside the River Forsa so navigation and fatigue would not be an issue. At the mouth of the Forsa I left the road to Craignure behind – the following day I would head that way to catch a ferry to the mainland at Oban. Now, though, I rumbled over cattle grids past what I presumed was the estate manager's cottage – the last habitable dwelling I would see on my journey into the glen.

The coastal road gave only a vague indication of the magnitude of these mountains; it is only when you travel deep into the heart of them that their size really sinks in. I felt miniscule and hugely insignificant at their feet; a mouse at the toes of giants. But it's the feeling of awe that would stay with me. Even in the low light I couldn't help but find this raw natural beauty remarkable. The highland cattle that littered the grass by the river around me seemed blissfully unaware of it all, nonchalantly chewing the cud and unfazed by my arrival. So unmoved were they, that the members of the herd standing on the trail ahead of me refused to budge, so I had no choice but to gingerly make my way through them, trying not to locate their eyes beneath their red shaggy manes or glance at horns that must span twice the width

of my shoulders. Mercifully they seemed strangely accepting of my passage, though I couldn't imagine they encounter humans often.

With their disappearance behind me seemed to go the last vestiges of civilisation; without them I began to feel utterly alone. The trail beneath these lesser mountains started to meander along with the river, and up ahead on the opposite bank I spotted two dilapidated huts. Thinking one might be Tomsleibhe I quickened the pace, before realising as I got closer that these must once have been dwellings until the clearances robbed them of their inhabitants. Now it looked like they were used for storage by the estate. As I paused by the footbridge that led over to them, scanning the mountain range that grew gradually in size as I neared my quarry, I spotted movement in the trees. The wingspan that unfolded as a bird took flight from the trees was huge – I could even tell from this distance – and the brown, white and gold colouring I noticed as it soared majestically over the huts could surely only belong to a golden eagle. I crouched down, my breath held in excitement, as I watched this glorious creature glide low over the glade. When it returned to the trees I waited, eager for its reappearance, but that was the last I saw of it, an airborne king of this wildest of places.

The pace of my final foray through the glen was more upbeat now. My feelings of isolation were banished, replaced by one of privilege, having witnessed such humbling natural beauty. The trail rose, and it was in the shadow of Beinn Talaidh that I found Tomsleibhe, my own personal hotel for the night. I dragged my bike through the fast flowing Forsa, trying to nimbly tiptoe across small stepping stones, and in the dwindling twilight opened its door to survey my lodgings. Unlike the Blair Atholl and Loch Lomond bothies, this one had a porch, hall and three bedrooms – two of which had working fireplaces. Thinking it would be easier to keep the smaller of them warm I brought bundles of firewood in from the porch, lit candles protruding from old champagne bottles (it must have been a strange yet wonderful party) and donned all my layers after noticing how cold I'd become now that I'd stopped moving.

A glowing hearth soon puts the world to rights, though, and in its light I scanned the pages of the bothy book. I could see no immediate common link between those who had left their musings in this book – exchange students, forestry workers, a shop assistant from Oban – but a love of Mull's wilderness must have united them all. I thought I'd found an entry from the champagne drinkers too – a father and son from Glasgow were there a fortnight before me to celebrate dad's fiftieth birthday. It may be a little way off, but when I reach that landmark I think it would be a wonderful way to mark such an occasion, riding back with my grown sons to raise a glass of bubbly to the passing of years well lived. What better way to foster a shared love of adventure than a memorable night in a far-flung cottage set deep in this wondrous glen?

After a traditional Scottish breakfast of porridge, and having gathered wood to replace what I'd used, I set off back along the trail the next morning to the coast knowing that I would see this otherworldly place again, and maybe I'd bring my own bottle to add to Tomsleibhe's collection of eclectic candlesticks.

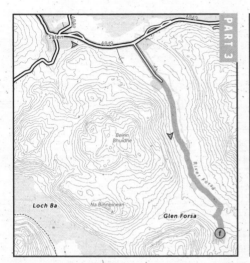

Salen

A849

A849

Beinn
Bhuidhe

River Forsa

Loch Ba

Na Binneinean

Glen Forsa

f

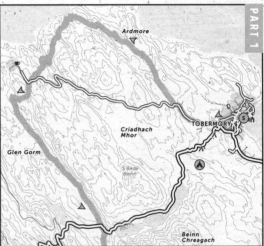

Ardmore

Criadhach
Mhor

Glen Gorm

S Airde
Beinn

TOBERMORY

S

Beinn
Chreagach

B8073

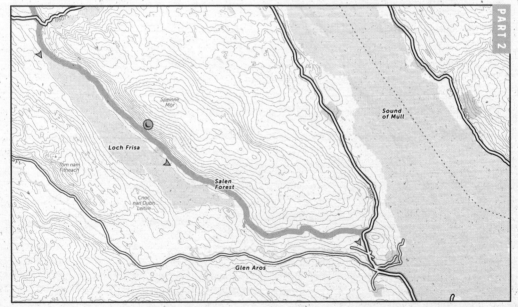

B8073

Speinne
Mòr

Sound
of Mull

Loch Frisa

Tòm nam
Fitheach

Salen
Forest

Cnoc
nan Dubh
Leitire

Glen Aros

BETWEEN A LOCH AND A HARD PLACE

THE WEST HIGHLAND WAY SNAKES ITS WAY PAST LOCHS AND PEAKS ALIKE ON THIS WILDEST OF BOTHY ADVENTURES

My love of bothy bikepacking led me to revisit the West Highland Way where it runs alongside Loch Lomond. The Highlands only seem to deal in superlatives – Loch Lomond is the largest body of water in Britain, Ben Nevis the highest mountain, the journey by rail surely the most beautiful – and continue to inspire awe and fascination in all who set foot or tyre here, myself included. I have ridden the entire 150km trail before, from Milngavie just north of Glasgow to Fort William, a regular venue on the UCI Downhill World Cup circuit. Laden with camping gear I was looking for something a little less gravity-assisted so focused on the middle section, where it runs beneath Ben Lomond and Ben Vorlich. There are two bothies on the loch shore – Rowchoish, opposite Tarbet and just north of Rob Roy's prison, and Doune Byre, 10km north of there, opposite Ardlui – and the West Highland Way runs right past their doorsteps.

INFO:

START: Arrochar and Tarbet station, G83 7DB, 56.203428, -4.722889
FINISH: Crianlarich station, FK20 8QN, 56.389634, -4.617805

DISTANCE: 21.5 miles/34.6km   **ASCENT:** 3421ft/1043m   **OFF-ROAD:** 90%

TERRAIN: Technical forest tracks, boulder fields and old military roads. Apart from the lower slopes of Ben Vorlich and the climb to Crianlarich it's relatively flat, along valley floors and loch-side paths.

NAVIGATION: Straightforward. The Three Lochs Way through Glen Loin is signposted from Arrochar and Tarbet station, with the Cowal Way joining it from the south-west. At Inveruglas Water make sure you don't follow the Cowal Way all the way into Inveruglas; look for two buildings where a track on the left takes you onto Ben Vorlich above the power station. The West Highland Way is well signposted and easy to pick up at Ardleish Farm pier. OS Landranger 56 covers most of the ride, except Crianlarich which can be found on Landranger 50.

EAT AND DRINK:

Village Inn, Loch Long, Shore Road, Arrochar, Argyll & Bute G83 7AX, 01301 702279, www.villageinnarrochar.co.uk
The Rod and Reel, Main Street, Crianlarich FK20 8QN, 01838 300271, www.rodandreel.co.uk

SLEEP:

Ardlui Hotel, Ardlui, Loch Lomond, G83 7EB, 01301 704243, www.ardlui.com
Beinglas Farm Campsite, Inverarnan, Loch Lomond G83 7DX, 01301 704281, www.beinglascampsite.co.uk
Doune Byre bothy, 56.292949, -4.696251

PROVISIONS:

Braeside Stores, Braemore, Arrochar, Argyll & Bute G83 7AA, 01301 702304
Helensburgh Cycles, 41 East Clyde Street, Helensburgh, Dumbartonshire G84 7NY, 01436 675239, www.helensburghcycles.co.uk

Rail access lies on the western shores, at Arrochar and Tarbet, Ardlui and further north at Crianlarich, where the River Falloch flows down into the loch. As such there were a number of routes open to me (my destination was Crianlarich) but it would involve a ferry crossing to get to the West Highland Way on the east bank. Cruise Loch Lomond run services from a number of piers along the loch (though some are summer only – check www.cruiselochlomond.co.uk) and initially I thought of crossing from Tarbet to Inversnaid, where a lovely old hotel, originally a hunting lodge for the Duke of Montrose, perches on the bank. There's also a great little bunkhouse there, halfway between Rowchoish and Doune Byre bothies, but although the trail south is relatively smooth, the section north to Doune Byre is a treacherous boulder field, with sheer shoulder-high rocks, which forced me to carry my bike for nearly 5 kilometres on my previous visit. As I needed to head north to continue my journey to the Western Isles I decided to ride from Arrochar and Tarbet to Ardlui, along forest trails and Ben Vorlich's lower slopes, and cross at Ardlui using the hotel's own ferry, making a short detour south from Ardleish Farm to Doune Byre bothy, before continuing on the West Highland Way to Crianlarich.

It was incredible how quickly the terrain changed as I left Glasgow. In less than 30km, Scotland's largest city had given way to small settlements punctuating the wilderness. And all the while mist-shrouded mountains rose majestically between the lochs. The line into Arrochar is sandwiched between three of them – Loch Long, Gare Loch and the southern stretch of Loch Lomond, where at its widest point it is 8km across.

The trail out of Arrochar was just as I'd pictured it; from the northern tip of Loch Long it ran north though a clearing between Kenmore Wood and Ardgartan Forest, giant pines forming a perfect corridor. It was a flat, hard-packed trail at first, but no path stays flat in the Highlands for long. Soon I was out of the saddle trying to winch myself up to Inveruglas Water, and from there climb nearly 150 metres up a wide path on Ben Vorlich's barren southern face. I was only a mere fraction of the way up the mountain, which falls just a handful of metres shy of Munro status (3,000ft/1,000m) but already the views of Loch Lomond and Ben Lomond behind (Scotland's most southerly Munro) were incredible. The weather had been mixed all day and a rainbow framed an already-perfect picture.

Thankfully I didn't need to climb any higher; instead a series of tight switchbacks sent me back to loch level again, and a short stretch of road led me north to Ardlui and my berth aboard the hotel's small ferry. Of all the bothies I have visited, I expected to have company for the night at Doune Byre; after all, the West Highland Way is one of Scotland's most popular long-distance paths, and was bound to still attract hikers and bikers at this late time in the year. However, as the ferry cast off under darkening skies, and shafts of sunlight pierced the clouds to create a dramatic backdrop to my flight across the loch, I realised I was the sole passenger for this short voyage. It was the last weekend in October, and from the following week until the beginning of April the ferry would only be available to hotel guests. I hadn't realised to what extent so many businesses in the Highlands close down out of season, but this was the third I'd heard of that day in its final week of operation before going into winter hibernation.

With the light fading dramatically during my brief foray across the water I was keen to locate the bothy before dark, so once off the Ardleish Farm pier I saddled up to locate the trail south. My recollection of the boulder field's extent must have been a little hazy, as it wasn't long before I was forced to dismount to pick my way along the rocky path. It certainly got worse further south, but the main problem here was the numerous channels running

across the path funnelling water down off the hills and into the loch. Many were more than a foot wide and some required stepping stones to get across. My progress was laboured but before long I spotted a glow some way along the trail. With no other habitation except the farm for miles, it must mean the bothy was already occupied. After a night isolated in the Cairngorms I was looking forward to some company so pressed on towards the light.

Inside the long, low building were a couple of twenty-somethings from Seattle and a local hiker maybe twice their age. It was relatively early but they already seemed to have hunkered down for the night. Still, they waved away my apologies for intruding and before long we were swapping stories of our travels and passing around a hip flask. Doune Byre must be one of the larger bothies; it is just a single hall with a sleeping platform covering one end, and two smaller ones by the hearth, and could easily have accommodated twice our number. The hiker told me he had already tried to find firewood but it had been raining for days so the tinder was sodden. Still, piping hot soup from my stove did the trick, and we continued chatting until the hip flask ran dry.

The next morning the Seattle couple were the first to leave. We said our farewells but continued to pass each other on the trail back north, as my progress for a while was no quicker than theirs. At a campsite bar, where a footbridge marks the intersection of loch and river, we eventually parted company, and my trail from there was challenging, though eminently rideable. Though the road and railway ran parallel to me on the other side of the River Falloch, the east bank felt incredibly wild still, a feeling enhanced by the sight of black feral mountain goats meandering across the trail ahead. After the wooded shelter of Doune it became bleak and exposed, and would stay that way until the forests which hide the small cluster of grey stone buildings that make up Crianlarich. You could almost picture how glaciers had rent and torn their way through this glen, however infinitesimally slowly, the peaks either side unchanged for countless millennia.

I heard the roar of the Falls of Falloch long before I saw the waterfall, its spray rising to join the mist that inevitably hung in this glen. A bridge at Derrydaroch guided the West Highland Way over to the Falloch's western bank, which soon ducked underneath both road and railway to join an old military road that began its ascent to the treeline of a dense pine forest. Crianlarich lay hidden behind the eastern fringe of the forest, and I ended this micro-adventure in much the same way I had started it, under a deciduous canopy. Yet the brutal Highland peaks had dominated this journey, by their sheer presence alone. A journey through these mountains is never to be taken lightly, and shelters such as Doune Byre and Rowchoish, however basic, make these adventures all the more achievable. Two weeks later, I learnt, the mountain hares in the area were waiting for their brown fur to catch up and change white to match their snow-bound surroundings. Seasons change quickly in the Highlands, and when they catch travellers unaware these bothies really come into their own. Without them I'd think twice about riding out on such epic Highland expeditions alone.

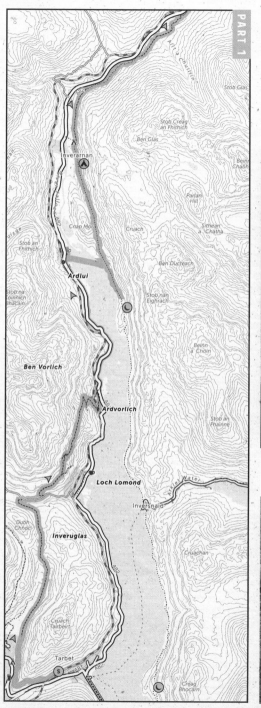

MOUNTAIN BIKES AND BOTHY NIGHTS

A NEAR FORGOTTEN BOTHY ABOVE BLAIR ATHOLL IN THE BLEAKLY BEAUTIFUL CAIRNGORMS PROMISES FANTASTIC WILD RIDING FROM ITS DOORSTEP

I was filled with apprehension as I disembarked at Pitlochry station. It had only taken me 90 minutes to reach this handsome Highland town from Glasgow's Queen Street station but the two places were worlds apart. The wooded valleys of the Tay and Tummel (Pitlochry perches on the banks of the latter) looked peaceful and inviting but the mountains that separate them were barren and inhospitable. From the valley floor they towered like brooding giants,

each crest reaching more than 500 metres above me, with the highest of them all, Farragon Hill at 783 metres, lurking menacingly behind a veil of mist.

Yet my nervousness didn't stem from the prospect of tackling these hostile-looking slopes; it was more from a feeling of venturing far into the unknown. I was, after all, embarking on my first bothy night, planning to hole up for the night in one of the many rudimentary shelters scattered across Scotland

---

INFO:

START: Pitlochry station, Station Road PH16 5AN, 56.702539, -3.735359
FINISH: Blair Atholl station, PH18 5SL 56.765464, -3.849634

DISTANCE: 31.8 miles/51.1km   **ASCENT:** 4196ft/1279m   **OFF-ROAD:** 85%

TERRAIN: Fire roads, forest trails, faint peat tracks and stony singletrack. There are long exposed climbs with brief respite in Baluain Wood and along the valley of the River Garry.

NAVIGATION: North of Blair Atholl is difficult. The trail beyond the bothy on day two is demanding, and difficult to follow. Cross the stream as close to the bothy as possible; climb north-west out of the Allt Scheicheachan valley and you should soon pick up the trail. Cross the Bruar River at Bruar Lodge. The later road sections are along NCN Route 7 so are well signposted, but OS Landrangers 43 and 52 could be useful companions.

EAT AND DRINK:

Bothy Bar, Blair Atholl Arms Hotel, Blair Atholl, Perthshire PH18 5SG, 01796 481205, www.athollarmshotel.co.uk
Mackenzie's Coffee House, 115 Atholl Road, Pitlochry PH16 5AG, 01796 470555, www.mackenziesofpitlochry.co.uk

SLEEP:

The Struan Inn, Calvine, Pitlochry, Perthshire PH18 5UB, 01796 483714, www.thestruan-inn.co.uk
Allt Scheicheachan bothy, 56.839702, -3.910970

PROVISIONS:

Atholl Grocery Stores, The Square, Blair Atholl, Pitlochry, Perthshire PH18 5TQ, 01796 481209
Escape Route, 3 Atholl Road, Pitlochry, Perthshire PH16 5BX, 01796 473859, www.escape-route.co.uk

and the north of England run by the Mountain Bothy Association. As I would find out during my journey through Scotland, they can vary immensely in size – from tiny single-room dwellings to large halls capable of accommodating a dozen or so weary bikers or hikers. Yet the premise of each one is the same: a shelter and safe haven from the elements, which in the Highlands especially can turn particularly cruel within minutes. Volunteer working parties keep them in good order, and travellers are asked to respect the bothy code, replenishing firewood when they can and perhaps leaving unwanted items such as canned foodstuffs, clothing and blankets that other visitors may be in need of. In many bothies, you'll even find a bothy book, which can contain years' worth of thoughts, comments and observations from those who have been before you. It makes you feel that you belong to some secret club, with a very select membership, when in reality bothies are open to all and really engender a sense of community between those who love the outdoors.

I couldn't wait to assuage my fears and find my shelter for the night – Allt Scheicheachan bothy, 8km north of Blair Atholl on the slopes of Glen Bruar, but first I needed to reach the little Highland village. I could have ridden north along a lonely stretch of road deemed quiet enough to be part of NCN route 7, which in its entirety runs from Sunderland to Inverness, but there were some delicious looking trails along the River Tummel and on the other side of Loch Faskally that I couldn't wait to explore, as well as the challenging ascent of Tulach Hill, from where the views would be breathtaking, if only the mist would clear. The trails lived up to my expectations – tight wooded singletrack hugging the loch shore all the way to the Pass of Killicrankie. Route 7 signs assured me of safe passage along the pass up to Blair Atholl, but I was keen to earn my dram of single malt at the bothy later that evening, so rolled over a bridge where

the Tummel meets the River Garry and began a road climb through pine trees glistening with moisture – either from recent rain or the mist that hung low along the valley.

Before long I was out of the trees and coasting past the isolated dwellings of Glen Fincastle. Those too soon gave way to the occasional cairn punctuating the scrub as I passed beneath Tulach Hill. If I thought this was exposed and isolated, I had another think coming on the trail out of Allt Scheicheachan. I was reassured by the sight of a distant train pulling into the outpost of Blair Atholl, and with the promise of fine views up here succumbing to the mist, I scrabbled down the scree-strewn valley slopes to the railway station's ancient signal box and level crossing.

This would be my ultimate destination the following day, but I lingered only long enough for a hot brew in the hotel's aptly named Bothy Bar before pressing on. Oddly enough my first encounter on my way up Banvie Burn was with crowds of visitors milling around Blair Castle, a 750-year-old medieval fortification that has slowly evolved into a magnificent example of Scottish baronial architecture. The ancestral seat of the Murrays of Atholl, it has now become a flagship exhibition venue and attraction thanks to a millennial project to construct the new Banvie Hall, but has lost none of its historic splendour.

I couldn't hide a rueful smile as I rode past the castle visitors, knowing they would all be retreating to the comforts of home as the evening started to draw in. My journey, however, took me on a riverside fireroad climb through Glen Banvie, along which the trees were dripping and the trail saturated, despite no rain having fallen since I had arrived. Then I was out of the trees and climbing out of the glen, and the world took on a different hue – the thick mist bleaching most of the colour from the scrub and bracken. A fierce wind began to whip at my hood now I had left the shelter of the trees behind, and beneath its

howl I could just about make out brief but repetitive noises, sharp and guttural. It was only when I saw the majestic silhouette, high up on Carn Dearg Mòr, that I could place the sound – a stag barking, a herd of red deer lurking not far behind. As my journey north was well into October I had just missed deer-stalking season, but on the advice of the Mountain Bothy Association had called the estate office to check it was safe to venture along the glen.

Light was fading fast, and my anxiety was heightening – I really didn't want to be out on these hills at nightfall. What if I couldn't find the bothy, or it was locked? I'd brought a tarp and bivvy in case of emergency but I really didn't want to resort to using those as my sole means of protection from the elements. As the deer finally sloped off the ridge above me I could just make out a ramshackle-looking hut sitting by the side of a stream. It must be Allt Scheicheachan, I realised, as I flicked up a gear and careened down the slope to the squat little bothy. My heart was in my mouth as I dismounted and leaned my bike against the wall. I tried the door, and felt an overwhelming sense of relief as it swung open on barely touching the latch (I learnt later that you'll never find a bothy locked, unless it is in dire need of repair, and even then updates on the MBA website will alert would-be visitors).

Allt Scheicheachan was a simple two-room dwelling, but it surpassed my expectations. Although one room was given over entirely to the storage of tools and fuel, the main compartment was welcoming, cosy even. Two sleeping platforms were covered by bed rolls, and a pair of benches sat close to the hearth. All around the room were items left by previous visitors – candles, gloves, a torch, tinned food and sachets of hot chocolate. My heart was warmed by the sight of a full coal bucket, and by comments left in the bothy book which I leafed through while getting the fire to take. The light had

disappeared outside now, and squally showers hit the windows with some force, as I examined the maps on the walls by torchlight. I thought how wonderful it is that these safe havens still exist, and welcome all travellers, serving to entice them onto the often foreboding but equally beautiful Scottish hills.

My journey the next day, up to Bruar Lodge (the nearest habitable dwelling for nearly 8km) and back along Glen Bruar's fireroad to the old military road at Calvine and through Baluain Wood back to Blair Atholl, would be at times difficult to navigate, isolated, exposed and exhausting yet ultimately hugely satisfying. Both the views and the descent from Gleann a' Chrombaidh would be exhilarating – the former of the Tay Forest Park's verdant expanse; the latter down a wide, flowing chalky trail. But for now I rewarded myself with that promised dram and toasted the volunteers of the MBA. Without their selfless efforts, I wouldn't be here riding in this beautiful, far-flung corner of the Cairngorms amid breathtaking wilderness, hardly touched by human hand. As the winds picked up outside and rattled the panes, I felt the warmth of the fire on my cheeks, and knew my next bothy night would not fill me with trepidation so much as a heightened sense of anticipation. Eventually I settled down in surprising comfort for the night, the dying flicker of the fire dancing on the bothy's stone walls.

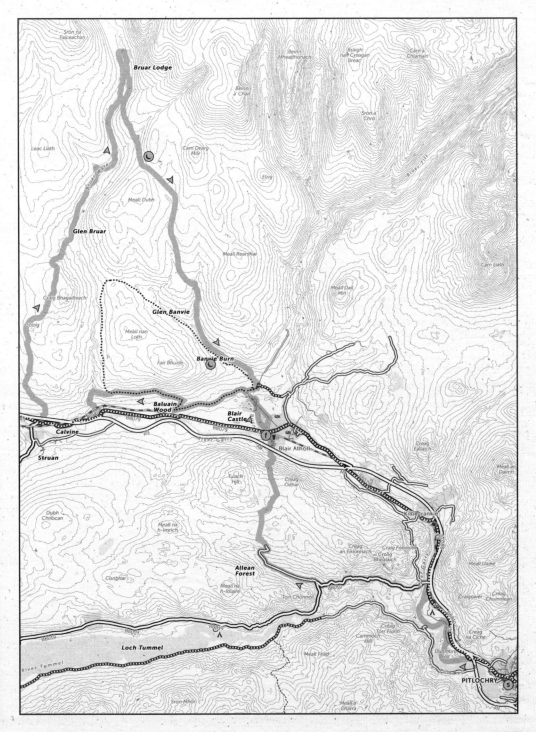

SURF'S UP

SURPRISINGLY, SUBLIME TRAILS ALONG THE GOWER PENINSULA'S HEADLAND AND SAND DUNES ARE JUST A RIDE AWAY FROM SWANSEA'S SEAFRONT

To many, the prospect of Welsh cross-country riding conjures up images of Snowdonia, the Black Mountains and the Brecon Beacons – epic in their proportions, and stern tests of a rider's fitness, endurance and handling skills. Much of my experience riding in Wales mirrors this – steep-sided wooded valleys, rolling hills and vast, exposed mountain tops. But there is another jewel in the crown of Welsh trail riding, and one often overlooked. Stretches of the country's coastline are among the most beautiful in the British Isles, and it was to one of its finest examples, Rhossili Bay

on the Gower Peninsula, that a Welsh friend and I headed to one early autumn morning.

We started our ride from another stretch of famous Welsh coastline, though the mudflats along Swansea's southern beachfront, while close to the Mumbles, did not hold the immediate appeal of our destination – the sandy crescent of Rhossili Bay overlooked by the steep, rugged downs. It does, though, have the city's only country park – Clyne Valley – and it was here that we parked our van, although Swansea's railway station is just a few miles away. There are some grand gated residences

---

INFO:

START/FINISH: Car park near Clyne Valley Country Park, SA3 5EQ, 51.598484, -4.002984

DISTANCE: 42.1 miles/67.7km   **ASCENT:** 4455ft/138m   **OFF-ROAD:** 70%

TERRAIN: A mixture of rock-strewn valleys and exposed downlands. There are occasional road climbs but Cefn Bryn and Rhossili Down provide the toughest off-road tests.

NAVIGATION: Fairly easy. The route is well signposted throughout. Follow the Gower Way signs over Cefn Bryn and round Rhossili Down. You should pick them up again near Llanrhidian as far as Three Crosses. The bridleway through Lake Farm at Llanddewi is easy to miss and on the return leg make sure you keep left along the top of Clyne Golf Course to avoid dropping down Clyne Common. OS Explorer 164 would be useful.

EAT AND DRINK:
Eddy's Café-Bar, Hillend Camping & Caravan Park, Hillend, Llangennith, Gower, Swansea SA3 1JD, 01792 386606, www.hillendcamping.com
Kings Head, Llangennith, Gower, Swansea SA3 1HX, 01792 386212, www.kingsheadgower.co.uk

SLEEP:
Rhossili Bunkhouse, Middleton, Rhossili, Swansea SA3 1PL, 01792 391509, www.rhossilibunkhouse.com
Bivvy: White Moor, Rhossili Down

PROVISIONS:
Pennard Stores & Coffee Shop, 68 Southgate Road, Southgate, Gower, Swansea SA3 2DH, 01792 233230, www.threecliffs.co.uk
The Bike Hub Cycle Workshop, 78 St Helens Road, Swansea SA1 4BQ, 01792 466944, www.thebikehub.co.uk

on the lane that climbs up along the south-west periphery of the park, but as the road turns to rough doubletrack they become fewer and further between and by the time our trail had disintegrated into a steep stone-strewn bridle path, we'd left all signs of habitation behind. Before long we emerged from a tunnel cut into dense copses of birch and beech, panting after such an early climb, onto the upper reaches of Clyne Common. From here we could already see Swansea Bay opening out behind us, and Mumbles Head at the tip of the crescent. While so close to Wales' second-largest city, the common, which lies at the edge of the Gower Area of Outstanding Natural Beauty, has a distinctly wild feel to it. Once a hive of industrial activity such as coal mining and brick making, the Clyne Valley now lies dormant, though a rich habitat has emerged from neglect to reclaim its slopes.

We followed a wisp of singletrack over the common and out onto one of the wildest golf courses I had ever seen. If it hadn't been for the occasional red flag or golf buggy I wouldn't even have noticed, so camouflaged were the fairways. The appearance of a wild pony or two did little to dispel the illusion of traversing a desolate moor top.

A track doubled back from the links course and soon we were plummeting off the downs, and picking our way through saturated fields as we headed for our first taste of the coast. After a dalliance with suburbia around Murton, we were faced with a sketchy descent into Bishopstone Valley, a secluded spot and silent save for the murmur of the river that runs down into Bantam Bay. Our route didn't allow us to enjoy the valley's peaceful wooded embrace for long as we were soon faced with a miniature boulder field up a twisting gully. Scattered stones the size of fists made it a demanding and technical climb, and eventually it was with a real sense of achievement that we emerged amid the throngs milling around the café at West Cliff.

Knowing what lay in wait for us an hour further along the trail, we took the opportunity to rest and refuel here too, before enjoying a leisurely spin across the clifftops to take in the sights of Three Cliffs Bay, and beyond it the golden sandy bays of Oxwich and Port Eynon, before heading inland, where the dunes of Pennard Burrows made our progress laboured and pedestrian. It wasn't long though before we were rumbling down a rocky chute to cross a wooden bridge over Pennard Pill, where our trail led us through a wooded valley and up onto clifftops once more, past a lovely little campsite that I'd stayed at before.

At last we were confronted by the huge, whale-like ridge of Cefn Bryn, along whose entire spine our trail would run. Though perhaps only a 100 metre gain in height, it was a torturous climb approaching from the east, and the expansive views that eventually rewarded us were hard won. We had an even better view of Port Eynon Bay below us, and over to the west the silhouette of Rhossili Down shielded its own sandy cove, and no doubt hordes of surfboarders, who flock there whatever the season. As we traversed the length of Cefn Bryn we were buffeted mercilessly by an unrelenting wind, and despite the ever-changing panorama that accompanied our ride across the ridge, we were relieved to drop down onto tarmac at last to coast through the villages of Reynoldston and Knelston.

As the afternoon sun started to dip low over Rhossili Down ahead, we rolled along rutted farm tracks as we ate up the miles in our bid to reach Rhossili Bay before sunset. I'd pictured us setting our tent up on the sea-facing slopes of the Down, but the wind had picked up so much that we both decided the more sheltered eastern face would be a better bet. As our trail gradually rose to meet the Downs we cut back across its marsh-like leeward slope in search of firmer ground. We were fortunate

to find our ideal spot just as the sun sank into the bay; we'd reached White Moor, almost at the Downs' northern tip and a stone's throw from the picturesque coastal village of Llangennith. The trail across the Downs was sodden and heavy going, but here beneath the scrub the ground was harder, and our pitch sheltered by brush and the remnants of a dry stone wall.

The tent was up in no time, and with a fire prepared we remounted and freewheeled down into Llangennith for a well-earned aperitif. Our visit to the popular village pub was longer than we planned, as we stayed to soak up the convivial atmosphere of the crowded bar, heaving with patrons to watch the national rugby team's televised World Cup quarter final. By the time we arrived Wales were already out, but the crowds still lingered, their conversations animated and jovial – of chances missed and luck running out. Soon we felt in need of a little respite from the hubbub, and headed outside to ride back up to our camp. In the welcome silence up on the downs we soon felt the warmth of the fire on our faces and soup in our bellies, and my companion produced two bottles of take-out he'd squirrelled back from the

pub. As the lights began to go out in the village below us, we kicked back and reflected on an occasionally taxing and technical journey to this beautiful bay. The following day would bring the return leg, a figure of eight that would let us dip our wheels in the sea on the southern shore at Oxwich before traversing Cefn Bryn once more across its axis, following the Gower Way round Swansea's airfield on Fairwood Common, before returning to the wild fairways on Clyne Common and from there, home.

First on the agenda, after we packed up camp and buried the ashes from last night, was a visit to Hillend campsite. Though the site was almost deserted, its renowned café, Eddy's, was doing a roaring trade, serving up generous breakfasts to non-residents. We filled our boots with a hearty Welsh breakfast, knowing that a steep slog up Rhossili Down awaited. I'd like to think I could have ridden up the harsh climb to Bessie's Meadow had I not overdone it with the fry-up, but the truth is it was so steep as to be un-rideable. It was a punishing push, but worth it, as at the ridge our quarry – Rhossili Bay and Worm's Head – unfurled before us. From this height we could just about make out a surf school being put through their paces on the beach in the bay as we followed the ribbon of singletrack along the Downs' length. An exhilarating descent delivered us into Rhossili village, where we followed the Gower Way to its logical conclusion – it finishes abruptly at the lookout station, from where only at low tide can you walk out onto Worm's Head. Sadly, we'd got our timing wrong, but in reaching this peninsula we agreed that we had discovered a very different aspect of Welsh riding, and with a 1,400km path spanning the country's entire coastline, it's one that we'll happily return to, time and again.

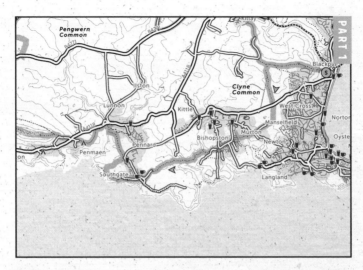

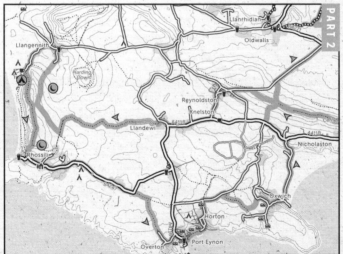

TOUCHING THE SKY

A MEMORABLE JOURNEY TO THE HIGHEST MOUNTAIN IN WALES, RIDING THROUGH SNOWDONIA'S SUBLIME LANDSCAPE FOR AN ATTEMPT ON THE SUMMIT ALONG THE RANGER'S PATH

My decision to climb Snowdon had been surprisingly spur-of-the-moment, coming during a week-long family camping trip to Dolgellau. There's nothing new in a ride up the Rhyd-Ddu, Snowdon Ranger or Llanberis paths, the three rideable routes to the summit, spectacular though they might be, so instead I decided to start my ride at the Welsh Highland Railway stop of Pont Croesor at Prenteg, while my children took the charming heritage steam engine to meet me back in Beddgelert. We were advised to book our tickets in advance, and although it was an expensive trip (return tickets between Caernarfon and Porthmadog can cost up to £36) kids ride for half price, and dogs and bikes can be booked for £3 each.

As I rolled out over the Glaslyn River on the B-road to Garreg, the children took their bikes and our collie on what is probably one of the most spectacular stretches of railway in Britain. My morning alone on the bike proved to be no less picturesque: I rode through Garreg, a lovely little hamlet where every house has violet window frames, towards

INFO:

START: Pont Croesor mountain railway station, LL49 9SP, 52.949518, -4.098102
FINISH: Snowdon summit, 53.069768, -4.075136

DISTANCE: 20.4 miles/32.8km   **ASCENT:** 5767ft/1758m   **OFF-ROAD:** 75%

TERRAIN: Quiet lanes, rutted paths and waymarked trails before the steady partially paved yet arduous route to the summit.

PUBLIC TRANSPORT: This ride does finish at the summit station, but sadly you can't take bikes on the train. However, there are three bridleway descents, two of which are very close to the mountain railway stations.

NAVIGATION: Surprisingly straightforward. With the Lôn Gwyrfai and Snowdon Ranger paths both waymarked, the trickiest sections are around Croesor and out of Pont Aberglaslyn, where you'll need to push up a footpath before you can remount as you turn right on a trail that runs across you. OS Landranger 115 could be useful.

EAT AND DRINK:

Snowdonia Parc Brewpub, Waunfawr, Caernarfon, Gwynedd LL55 4AQ, 01286 650409, www.snowdonia-park.co.uk

Hebog Cafe and Bistro, Beddgelert, Caernarfon, Gwynedd LL55 4UY, 01766 890400, www.hebog-beddgelert.co.uk

SLEEP:

Bryn Gwynant YHA, Nant Gwynant, Caernarfon, Gwynedd LL55 4NP, 0845 371 9108, www.yha.org.uk

Snowdonia Parc campsite, Waunfawr, Caernarfon, LL55 4AQ, 01286 650409

Bivvy: Llyn Ffynnon-y-gwas

PROVISIONS:

Beddgelert Post Office and Store, Caernarfon Road, Beddgelert, Gwynedd LL55 4UY, 01766 890201

Beddgelert Bikes, The Bike Barn, Beddgelert, Caernarfon, Gwynedd LL55 4YW, 01766 890434, www.beddgelertbikes.co.uk

Croesor, with the woods thickening on one side and a waterfall cascading down the slopes on the other. Crossing over a dismantled railway at Croesor, just a sparse collections of stone dwellings, the road soon gave up the ghost, the tarmac giving way to loose stone until the byway turned into little more than a faint path across rough grazing pasture. Dropping into woodlands, I heard the steam engine's faint whistle echoing through the valley before I saw the highland railway station of Nantmor up ahead. The road took me over the railway line, which disappeared into the cliff before emerging along the Pass of Aberglaslyn, a beautiful gorge where the road and railway seemed to cling to either side of the river for the few kilometres up to Beddgelert. Though it's a relatively quiet A-road, it was not the way I planned to get there; instead I crossed both river and road and dismounted to climb through Aberglaslyn Woods on a steep footpath. Emerging from the trees, the upper slopes of Moel Hebog loomed ahead of me. Heading north I took in the jagged skyline of crags and peaks that led up to the largest of all, and my ultimate destination, though Snowdon's summit was shrouded in mist that morning.

The rough-hewn bridleway took me gently down the foothills of Moel Hebog to re-join my group at Beddgelert station. According to legend, the town is the resting place of Gelert, the faithful hound of medieval welsh prince Llewelyn the Great. Our own hound seemed quite at home here as we rode into Beddgelert Forest along the Lon Gwyrfai trail. My boys chattered with a mixture of excitement and relief as we rode along the valley floor between these imposing mountains – at times we could see Cadair Idris silhouetted behind us – and seeing them soaking up the sight of the largest mountains they have ever seen while cycling up them was an wonderful experience for me. We rode alongside the railway line for at least an hour, the train winding

in and out of clearings in the forest; we could hear the train returning towards us from Caernarfon long before we saw it. When we did, it was settled at Meillionen station, little more than a campsite with its own halt on the line, seemingly exhaling a cloud of its own vapour. The boys returned the waves of a family in the glass observation car on the front before we pressed on, crossing over the line and running no more than a few metres parallel to it before crossing again and darting back into the woods. We were alone in the hushed, verdant pines for some time before emerging by Llyn-y-Gader lake, and the epic panorama unfolded once more. These splintering crags were indeed daunting and are perhaps a little unsettling for youngsters, but I harboured hopes that if we returned one day they would join me in riding up Snowdon's slopes with the same sense of anticipation I was feeling. I unpacked my dry-bag and rustled up hot chocolates on my stove as we sat on the shore for a while and took it all in. We had time to kill before the next mountain train would take us up to Waunfawr for an early supper at a fantastic brewpub on a campsite there. We headed across a wooden walkway that skirted round the lake and pedalled up to the main road to Rhyd Ddu station.

After a light supper at Waunfawr I again set off alone. A voluntary cycle ban is in place on the Snowdon bridleways, excluding bikes from the mountain between 10am and 5pm between May and September, but this still gave me a few hours' daylight to find a good camp for the night. It was a fair slog on the road to get back to the Ranger Path, but worth it for the microbrewery's wonderful craft beer that helped steel my nerves for this testing climb.

Reaching the Snowdon ranger station, I was glad to leave the tarmac behind, even though an incredibly steep slope loomed large ahead. Fortunately a series of switchbacks mitigated the initial

hike in gradient before the stony path straightened out, snaking diagonally up the slope. It wasn't long before I was cursing my inability to turn down a good beer, because after riding perhaps 1,500 metres to the junction of the Ranger and Bwlch Maesgwm paths, the path had risen 250 metres, and every one had been a struggle. While the Bwlch Maesgwm heads north to Llanberis, I stuck to the summit-bound Ranger Path, rumbling over the rain bars that channel water off the trail and climbing steadily to the dry stone walls of old sheepfolds.

Dismounting to open the gate gave me the chance to catch my breath and as I rolled out along a grassy plateau I spotted the reservoir beside which I had planned to camp that evening. The basin in which Llyn Ffynnon-y-gwas sits is not too much a needless drop in height, and shallow enough to afford wonderful panoramic views, and as I headed down to the water's edge I could see a small overhang that appeared almost tailor-made for a night's wild camping. I needn't have worried about shelter though, because conditions had been improving all day, and although the mist kept hiding then revealing the summit, the sky, or what little there seemed to be of it above the encroaching peaks, was a clear pale blue.

It was perhaps the most beatific moment of all my wild camping exploits, as the last of the sun's rays turned the previously desolate, almost hostile Snowdon slopes into something altogether more benevolent, as I hunkered down against the chill. The Ranger Path above me had long since quietened; I presumed every single soul by now had come down off the mountain either by foot, bike or rail and I had dozens of lofty square kilometres all to myself – well, except for the sheep. And even when wolfing down my piping hot porridge the following morning, in awe of the beauty of the

wildest of sunrises, I knew it would be another few hours before I had any company.

Before my breakfast had even settled I was shaken out of my morning reverie, having to swing the bike round a series of switchbacks, with the surface loosening and the trail becoming increasingly technical. In fact, though it must make a wonderful descent, I found it un-rideable in places, yet felt no shame in pushing my bike up the unforgiving gradient. As the ridgeline revealed itself to me I saw what might be the first train of the morning making its methodical progress to the summit station, and soon I was back on my bike as the gradient levelled off, past the warning signs on the railway intersection, and with gritted teeth and lowest gear, I spun my way up the final ramp that runs parallel to the rails.

The final series of jagged rocks interrupting the thinnest of bridleways forced me to walk the last few hundred metres, and as I leaned my bike against the café wall beneath the most fitting of inscriptions (at 1,085 metres, the highest point in the British Isles outside the Scottish Highlands) – "Here we are closer to heaven" – I poked my head through this most conspicuous of cafeterias and was confronted with dozens of day-trippers fresh off the train, queuing up for overpriced coffee. I exited swiftly, choosing instead to be buffeted by the wind outside and planning to make my own brew on my way back down. I didn't have long before the curfew kicked in but I allowed myself long enough to marvel at the dramatic landscape beneath me, noticing with surprise and concern a yellow mountain rescue helicopter hovering over one of Snowdon's many lakes, hundreds of feet below me. With that I remounted and set about sampling Snowdon at a much quicker pace on the descent.

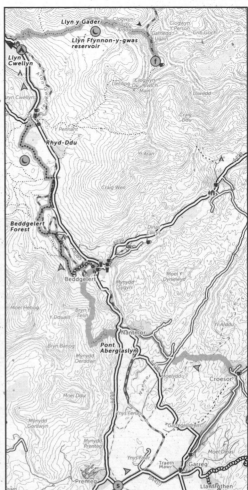

BREAK FOR THE BORDER

A RIDABLE OFF-ROAD ALTERNATIVE FOLLOWS THE OFFA'S DYKE PATH ALONG THE WELSH BORDER, WITH THE NORTHERN HALF TACKLING THE CLWYDIAN RANGE AND BERWYN HILLS

Riding in the Welsh mountains has a beauty all of its own; there's no mistaking the rugged hills and rolling valleys, vast in proportion and occasionally brutal in nature. It's a landscape that calls to long-distance riders and begs to be traversed in its entirety; a seemingly gargantuan feat to match the epic terrain. It's not surprising then, that a number of long distance routes have been forged across both axes – the trans-Cambrian Way, Sarn Helen and Taff Trails, for example. A friend and I had for some time been mulling over how best to plot a north-south, coast-to-coast ride until a mutual acquaintance came up with a route for a group ride that closely followed Offa's Dyke Path – predominantly a walking route – but using off-road tracks, bridleways and byways for the greater part of the 285km route from Prestatyn to Chepstow.

Due to the very nature of the route (King Offa built a system of earthworks in the 8th century to divide the English and Welsh), it follows the English-Welsh border closely, and traverses several Areas of Outstanding Natural Beauty such as the

---

INFO:

START: Prestatyn seafront LL19 7US, 53.341439, -3.411800
FINISH: White Horse Inn, The Square, Clun, Shropshire SY7 8JA, 52.421266, -3.029831

DISTANCE: Day one 51.5 miles/82.9km. **Day two** 68.2m/109.7km
ASCENT: Day one 7785ft/2373m. **Day two** 6794ft/2071m   **OFF-ROAD:** 65%

PUBLIC TRANSPORT: If the trans-Wales route (Offa North and Offa South) is ridden as a whole, there are train stations at both ends. If done separately, Broome station is 11km from Clun, the end point of this particular ride.

NAVIGATION: The length of this ride can cause some difficulties. All the bridleways are well signposted but GPS navigation is recommended to keep you on track across the Clwydian and Berwyn hills. OS Landranger 137, 126 and 116 would be helpful.

EAT AND DRINK:

The Druid Inn, Ruthin Road, Llanferres, Denbighshire CH7 5SN, 01352 810225, www.thedruidinn.com
The Royal Oak Hotel, The Cross, Welshpool, Powys SY21 7DG, 01938 552217, www.royaloakwelshpool.co.uk

SLEEP:

Youth hostel, Llangollen, www.llangollenhostel.co.uk
Bivvy: Wern Isaf wood near Castell Dinas Bran

PROVISIONS:

Oriel Bodfari Gallery, Cafe and Grocery, Mold Road, Bodfari LL16 4DN, 01745 710703, www.orielbodfarigallery.co.uk
Oneplanet Adventure, Coed Llandegla Forest, Ruthin Road, Llandegla, Denbighshire LL11 3AA, 01978 751656, www.oneplanetadventure.com

Clwydian Range and Dee Valley, Shropshire Hills and Wye Valley, but also the Berwyn Hills, the Black Mountains and Brecon Beacons.

My preparations for this, the longest off-road ride I have undertaken, were thorough, and as a group of five we decided we'd be better off staying in a lodge, hostel or pub rather than carry camping equipment throughout arduous day-long rides of 80-100km with an average of 2,000 metres off-road climbing each day. What we'd miss out on, unable to camp out in the mountains, we'd make up for in recuperation for the next day's efforts. Besides, we'd be immersed in beautiful Welsh hills, valleys and countryside for 10 hours a day, with plenty of opportunity to appreciate our surroundings.

So, at the beginning of the finest spell of weather Wales had seen all year, we rode out from our rendezvous in Prestatyn, eager to put some miles on the board and leave this tired coastal backwater behind. A post signalling the beginning of the Offa's Dyke Path also denoted the start of our route, and having studied the route profile we made the most of our flat departure from the coast, spinning steadily to warm up.

After a brisk climb at Gronant, the gradient toyed with us for a while, gently rising and falling through outlying villages and dipping to the road at Dyserth and Rhuallt before the Clwydian Range rose up in earnest, hedgerow-lined bridle paths winding up around its slopes. Before we knew it, the stony byways of the Clwydian Way had taken us to 300 metres above sea level, with views down to the lush green valley below. Prestatyn's hazy coastline was only now beginning to disappear from view, and we pressed on, amused by signs that we were entering the hamlet of Sodom, along a rare stretch of track where our route and the actual Offa's Dyke Path coincided.

Our track became more broken and technical as the Clwydian Way broadened, and it was clear when we reached Moel Arthur, the site of an Iron Age hillfort (around what's thought to be a Bronze Age burial mound), that we had gained yet more height. Now with this wealth of unspoilt country-side at our feet, we couldn't help but realise that although the world around us may have changed immeasurably since these earthworks were con-structed, the views of this serene landscape must have altered little.

We stopped to rest and refuel at a little pub at Llanferres, before enjoying some respite along the road at the foot of the now dwindling Clwydian Range. Our route avoided the harsh slopes of the Maesyrychen mountain, and we opted for the leafy expanse of Llandegla Forest, a mountain bikers' playground with a café and bike park at its trailhead. We enjoyed some flat-out riding along technical forest singletrack before descending along a steep, rocky pass between the sheer slopes of Eglwyseg and Ruabon mountains to Llangollen.

I instantly recognised our base for the night from childhood holidays spent across the border from our old Shrewsbury home. After changing at our hostel and heading out to town for supper, we crossed the bridge over the Dee, with Llangollen's lovely little train station sandwiched between the river and canal in the background.

The following morning, someone was playing the upright piano in the hostel's common room as we came down to breakfast, ready to fuel the day's journey to Clun. It was only when we found ourselves ordering second helpings last night that we realised just how many calories we must have burned up, and we knew that the next part of the route would be even longer. While Offa's Dyke Path skirts round the steep-sided valley of Glyn Ceiriog to the east, we started by heading

westward through rolling countryside, before swinging around and meeting briefly with the long distance path on the English side of the border at Rhydycroesau near Oswestry.

Quiet roads ate up the miles to Pen-y-Bont, where we followed the course of the Afon Tanat before the Llangollen Canal, a branch of the Shropshire Union Canal, guided us effortlessly through the Severn Valley and into Welshpool. The town's canal-side industry was a shock to the system after a morning spent riding across peaceful border lowlands. The canal stretches out for miles at a time without passing a dwelling of any kind, but here we were spoiled for choice where refreshments and supplies are concerned. The flat, unwavering path that we followed for more than 30km would have helped us keep a good tempo had it not been for the fresh-cut hawthorns that lay in wait to snare us. On half a dozen occasions our progress was hampered by canal-side puncture repairs. We left the dry, dusty towpath of what is now the Montgomery Canal, crossing a magnificent wrought iron bridge over the Severn at Abermule, before following another watercourse – this time the Afon Miwl – almost as far as Sarn. Here we picked up the Caebitra River for a while and coasted past a patchwork of green and yellow fields back into England.

Before long our tired legs felt the pull of the hills once more. We rode in a ragged line across faded plains, leaving plumes of dust in our wake, before joining the low slopes of the Shropshire Hills. Our energy levels were severely depleted and the slowly setting sun seemed to exacerbate our exhaustion. However, as we crossed the River Unk at Bicton through the valley, we made out the ruined ramparts of Clun's Norman castle clinging to the side of its mound, a sight that proved incentive enough for one final push. By now the only light in the sky emanated from this bustling market town. Friday night at the inn where we were staying – a carrot at the end of a stick half the length of Wales – seemed to be in full swing as we arrived, yet we dismounted wordlessly and slumped in varying states of exhaustion on its front steps, barely noticing customers stepping gingerly round us on their way to the bar. Eventually we composed ourselves and retreated to the only empty table, well-earned ales coming before a hearty meal.

After lambasting the Welshpool canal-side hedge trimmers, we pored over route maps and ride data. It had been an epic ride by any of our standards – and we had an ultramarathon runner in our midst! Having burned more than twice as many calories as we'd usually consume in a day went some way to explaining our fatigue, combined with our lack of recovery from the day before. At times it had felt like a slog, but the Welsh countryside in all its varying beauty had been our constant companion, somehow alleviating our suffering in the hills. A wonderful journey in its own right, we remained intent on continuing our path alongside Offa's earthworks all the way to Chepstow. We were halfway there, but the Brecon Beacons and Black Mountains awaited us...

(See the next chapter for the continuation of this trans-Wales ride inspired by the Offa's Dyke Path from Clun to Chepstow.)

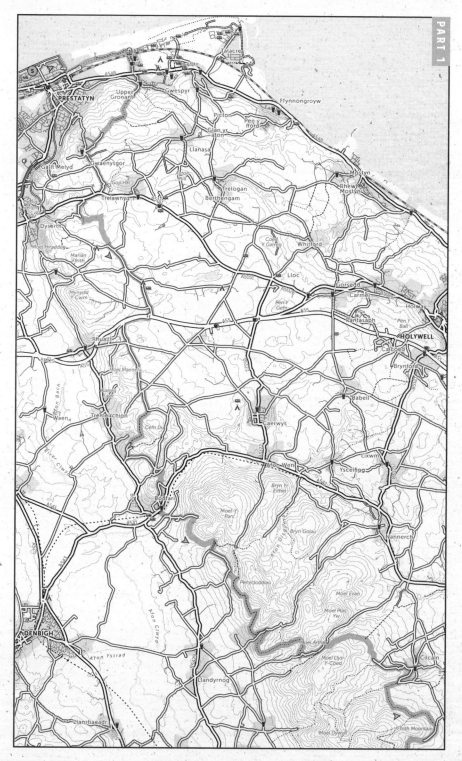

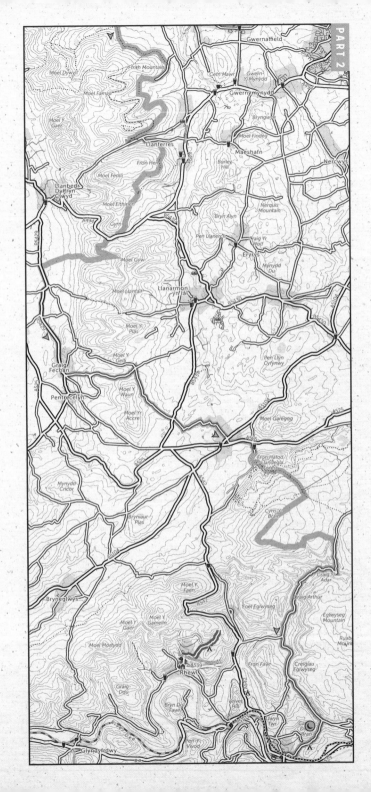

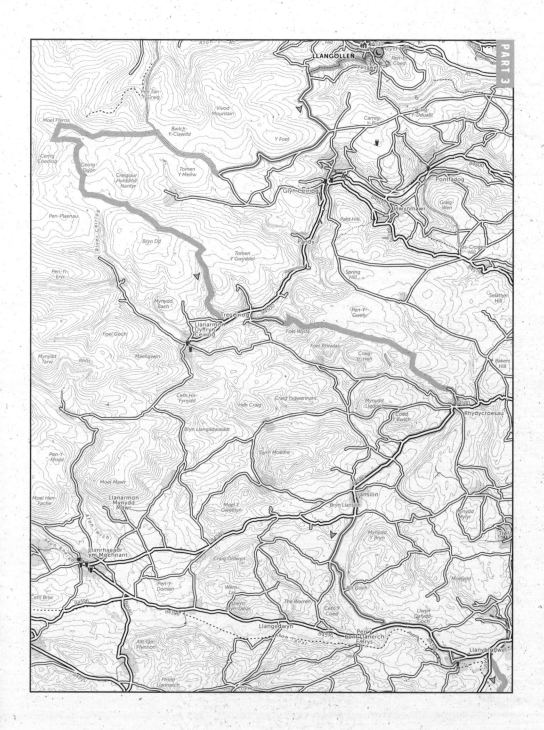

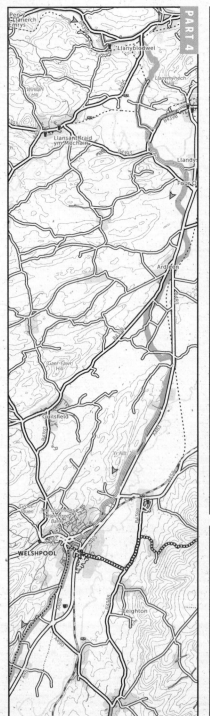

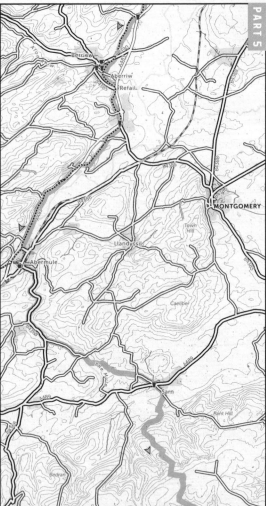

ALONG THE EDGE OF THE REALM

FROM THE SHROPSHIRE HILLS THIS EPIC OFF-ROAD ADVENTURE CHASES THE KING OF MERCIA'S ANCIENT EARTHWORKS SOUTH OVER THE BLACK MOUNTAINS TO THE WYE VALLEY

Our journey from Clun, through the Black Mountains, past the Brecon Beacons and eventually following the Forest of Dean's western treeline to our destination in Chepstow, is the second half of a mammoth trek along the length of Wales that I took with a group of cyclists. Our path rarely strayed more than a few miles from the largest earthworks in the UK – Offa's Dyke, built by the King of the Mercians 1,200 years ago to repel the Welsh from the English border. No comparable construction project would take place for another 1,000 years until the great canal schemes of the 18th century.

Though there are significant gaps along its length, in most parts the earth bank and often the ditch on the western side are still visible, with a long-distance path tracing its entire length, from Prestatyn on the River Dee to Chepstow on the Wye estuary. This ride follows Offa's footsteps as closely as possible, riding a parallel route across this untameable country that

---

INFO:

START: White Horse Inn, The Square, Clun, Shropshire SY7 8JA, 52.421266, -3.029831
FINISH: Offa's Dyke marker, Sedbury, 500m southeast of NP16 7HD, 51.632523, -2.648501

DISTANCE: Day one 49.6 miles/79.7km. **Day two** 61.8m/99.5km

ASCENT: Day one 6686ft/2038m. **Day two** 7211ft/2198m   **OFF-ROAD:** 55%

TERRAIN: Rough, grassy slopes, stony bridle paths and dirt tracks, and quiet road segments. Very hilly with more than 4,000m of climbing.

PUBLIC TRANSPORT: If the trans-Wales route (Offa North and South) is ridden as a whole, there are train stations at both ends. If done separately, Broome station is 11km from Clun, the start point of this particular ride.

NAVIGATION: Fairly straightforward. The length of this ride can make navigation an arduous task, though bridleways are easy to spot and the Jack Mytton Way is waymarked. Hay Bluff and Harley Dingle are the most difficult to negotiate. GPS navigation is recommended for those without strong map-reading skills. OS Landranger 161, 171, 148 and 137 would make very useful companions.

EAT AND DRINK:

Hunters Moon Inn, Llangattock Lingoed, Abergavenny, Gwent NP7 8RR, 01873 821499, www.hunters-moon-inn.co.uk
The Harp Inn, Glasbury-on-Wye, Powys HR3 5NR, 01497 847373, www.theharpinn.co.uk

SLEEP:

Black Mountain Lodge, Glasbury-on-Wye, Powys HR3 5PT, 01497 847779, www.blackmountainlodge.co.uk
Bivvy: on the edge of the wood near Moity

PROVISIONS:

The Maltings Tea Rooms, 12 High Street, Clun SY7 8JQ, 01588 640539, www.caryscakes.com
Drover Cycles, Forest Road, Hay-on-Wye HR3 5EH, 01497 822419, www.drovercycles.co.uk

meanders in places to cover over 300km from coast to coast. This southern section, though, is an epic ride all of its own and would make a challenging wild weekend for those into adventure riding.

Clun proved an ideal base from which to kick off the second stage of our journey. The luxury of a comfortable bed at the White Horse Inn may not be wild camping, but it gave us a chance to recuperate, with 130km under our belts already, and faced with another 180km over the next two days. The rugged terrain had taken its toll on our bikes, but that morning they required only minor adjustments that we could administer ourselves. There was a latent heat to the morning as we left Clun's market square and Norman castle behind, and rode out south-west towards the distant Black Mountains, initially along the Jack Mytton Way, which runs from the Wyre Forest to the Shropshire-Powys border.

The long-distance path let us gain steady height on the road, before we continued along the same contour on wide, dusty bridle paths that hooked round Llanfair Hill, already at 432 metres, to re-join Offa's Dyke. The earthworks were our constant companion, never far away, occasionally disappearing from view yet at other times towering up to eight metres above us. The dyke's linear path runs south-east to Knighton, where a museum heralds its half-way point, whereas we followed the Jack Mytton Way on a stony trail, then a narrow lane, to its end on the border at Lloyney.

From this moment on, at this picturesque hamlet straddling the River Teme, we called upon ever-dwindling energy reserves, at first climbing nearly 200 metres in less than 2km up onto the sepia slopes of Wernygeufron Hill. From there we followed the line of a railway that cut through the valley below us, before dropping to traverse it near Llanbister Road station. Our path took us beneath Radnor Forest's coniferous canopy and along a precarious path

atop the huge 4km-long crevice of Harley Dingle. Glascwm was the only outpost for miles as we rode across isolated but bleakly beautiful hill tops, and it was here that a dried-up rocky river bed rendered one of our bikes asunder – a snapped rear axle forced its pilot to walk down off the hills, and the rest of us to carry wheels and frame strapped to our day packs.

Fortunately we had already begun our descent into Glasbury along the Wye Valley so our bike-less companion had only a couple of kilometres to pick his way in cleated shoes down the tight, technical trail, while the rest of us shot down with reckless abandon. As we made our piecemeal descent, one of our group more familiar with the Black Mountains pointed out the twin escarpments of Hay Bluff and Lord Hereford's Knob, foreboding twin ridges that would await us the following morning. We were on the west, Welsh side of Offa's Dyke, which runs through nearby Hay-on-Wye, while a lodge on Glasbury's leafy outskirts, overlooking the Wye valley would play host to us that evening.

The following morning, while the group readied themselves for our final leg, I rode into Hay with the broken axle in a bid to find a replacement. In doing so I rediscovered how helpful small, independent bike shops can be. A little gem of a place on Wye's outskirts opened early on a Sunday especially for me, the owner keen to hear about our trans-Wales expedition as she sourced a replacement part. I re-joined the others outside the lodge, zipped up against the morning chill, and we rode out to the meet the day's nemesis, Twmpa (as Lord Hereford's Knob is known on this side of the border). Riding up to the foot of its harsh scarp face, from where the Black Mountains heave and roll south as far as Crickhowell and Abergavenny, there was a noticeable nervousness to our conversation. Our path passed underneath

Lord Hereford's impassive gaze, almost 400 metres above us, and as we rode round the barren escarpment of Hay Bluff we noticed our path – a sliver of stony singletrack – winching its way up to the ridgeline. The clunking of five chains simultaneously dropping into granny rings signalled the start of our endeavour, and after just a few minutes each of our party has stopped to strip off layers, before continuing to crawl slowly up the slope.

Joining the others slumped over their bars at the top, I noticed the Offa's Dyke Path running across the ridgeline, and the border, to the horizon, and for once we found ourselves on the 'English' side of the dyke, dropping down an exhilarating rocky chute to follow stony tracks halfway up the Olchon Valley. To the south, as we rode out of the valley over the River Monnow, what seemed like a metropolis began to appear – yet it was testimony to how remote we had been that the towns of Abergavenny, Blaenavon and Ebbw Vale seemed so grand. Over the railway tracks we stumbled upon another welcome example of Welsh hospitality, at a lovely old pub at Llangattock. Seeing five exhausted mountain bikers collapse around one of his garden tables, the landlord cajoled his chef into reopening his kitchen and before long we were topping up depleted energy reserves with steak baguettes and huge bowls of chunky chips.

Feeling somewhat restored, we headed out along our path alongside the dyke, which took us east through quiet and lonely vales, interspersed by small wooded clusters and a scattering of farmsteads, before riding into the bustling market town of Monmouth. With the Black Mountains and Brecon Beacons behind us, our remaining journey would be along grassy plains and wooded valleys along the River Wye. While the King of the Mercians' monumental feat of engineering was meant to keep out the Welsh, our parallel path gave us a glimpse of what riding in Wales is all about, even though at times some of the most inviting rides lay tantalisingly out of reach to the west. We often felt belittled by this wild and rugged landscape, yet riding its length from the mouth of the Dee to that of the Wye had certainly helped me connect with it somehow, and I began to anticipate the flow of the land here, how the terrain rolled, dipped and rose, and how the wooded valleys yielded to exposed hilltop scrub.

It was the former that eased our passage home, and before long we saw the magnificent archways of Tintern Abbey rising across the river. It was interesting to chat to a couple of hikers who were nearing the end of their own Offa's Dyke odyssey, and whose experiences mirrored ours. They had witnessed the landscape unfurl at a slower pace, had seen the minutiae that we had missed, though we joked that perhaps we had felt the landscape in a way that thankfully they had not! We joined them on the final stretch, where we had no choice but to trundle over wooden footbridges, bikes hiked up on back wheels, sharing the final footpath which wound its way up to Offa's Dyke marker. This monument celebrates not only the achievements of those like ourselves, who have completed this adventurous coast-to-coast route, but also the legacy of an ancient construction meant to divide nations that instead has become a source of common ground for those with an adventurous spirit.

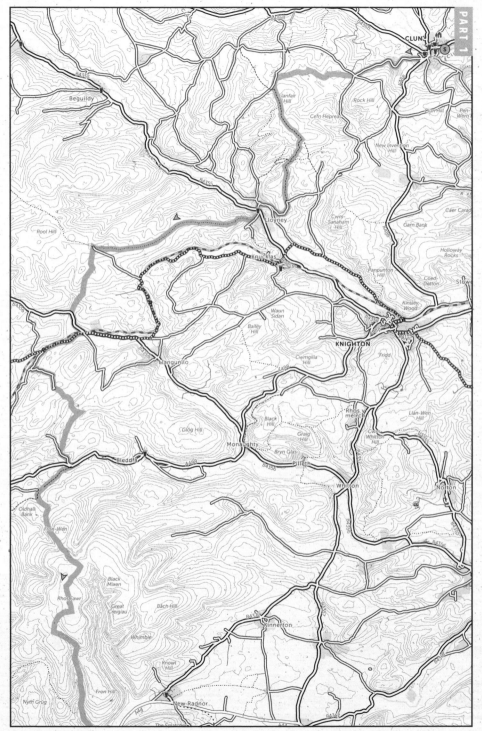

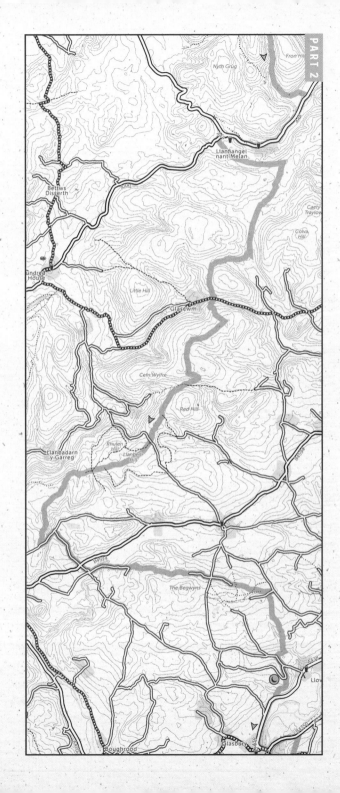

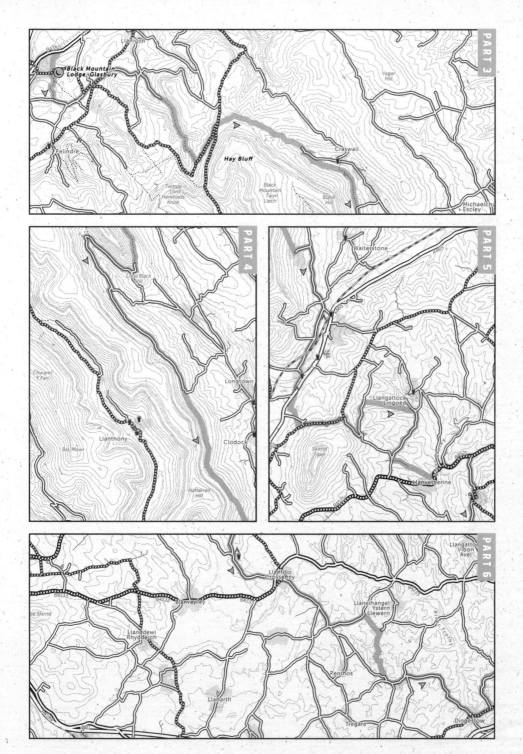

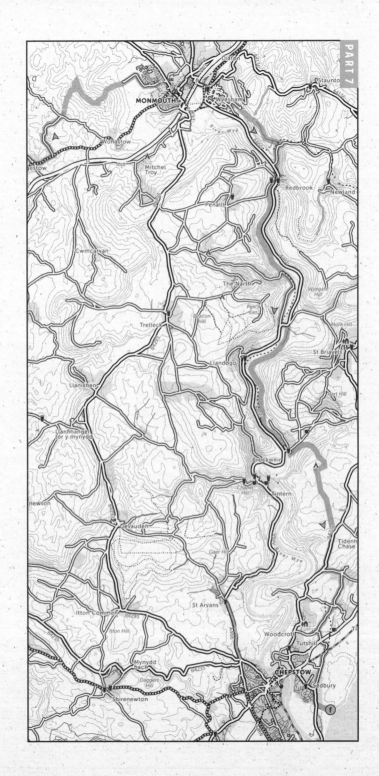

EPILOGUE

The history of mountain biking is so far a brief one, and fortunately so because we can still draw inspiration from its early pioneers – men like Gary Fisher, who is still a huge figurehead of the sport. Back in the 1970s they were long-haired kids with a devil-may-care attitude, a lust for life and a love of the raw wilderness of Marin County. In building their first Clunkers they sowed a seed imbued with that vitality and wanderlust that in this country is only now starting to germinate.

Bikepacking has become the perfect antidote to our manic modern existence. With our ever more introspective lifestyles leading us to become distanced from our green spaces and wild places, and bureaucracy and elitist land ownership often disenfranchising us, it's no surprise we've become ambivalent towards our natural environment. Our hectic, stressful, routine-driven lives do not lend themselves to leisurely exploration these days, yet they can't quench the thirst for adventure we sometimes feel either. We haven't lost our natural curiosity so much as misplaced it.

Those that embrace the outdoors, be they walkers, rock climbers, horse riders or mountain bikers, remember a secret than many others have forgotten, or never knew – that the rural landscape, which has come to seem alien to a nation of town and city dwellers, can hold the key to the most precious things: health and a sense of well-being, an opportunity for greater perspective, peace of mind and appreciation of the natural world around us, and a chance to breathe the freshest of air and take stock of things. It also holds the liberating opportunity for unadulterated escapism.

Wild riding, adventure biking, bikepacking – call it what you will; it's a magnificent way to reconnect with Britain's bountiful wilderness. Ours is an island of moors, mountains and rugged coasts; of plains, dense forests and glacial valleys. We just need to remove ourselves from our urban landscape once in a while to remember how wild and beautiful the British Isles are. Riding its wild trails and sleeping in its silent embrace is the most gratifying process of discovery, and one that stimulates each and every sense.

Coasteering, geocaching and enjoying microadventures are all concepts that seek to reinvent how we see and interact with our natural surroundings, and bikepacking follows in their footsteps. By its very nature mountain biking lets us explore the wilds as far away as our legs can carry us, so it's only natural, I suppose, that its marriage to wild, minimalist camping allows us to set our sights further still, rediscovering our rural surroundings and ultimately unveiling the remote wild places beyond. It's a hugely satisfying physical act – cresting arduous climbs, nailing technical descents and sometimes covering epic distances – but it satiates other latent desires too, scratching a primordial itch as we breath the heady scent of wood smoke, feel raw heat on our faces and lie with an unfettered view of the night sky, mid-way through a self-supported journey across a land that is ours at heart, if not by rights.

Pared back to its bare bones, bikepacking is a simple act of discovery, adventure and escapism, and anyone with a working bike, a rucksack and sleeping bag, and a few hours to spare can experience it. No matter how time-poor we have become, with a little lateral thinking we can always make time for a fat-tyred microadventure. You'd be surprised how many natural trails lie on your doorstep, or at least a short train ride away. Go on – dig out that local OS map, locate your home and trace a line to the nearest hills. When your day is done, why not just pack a bag or two, put some lube on your chain and head for them. You could even head straight to work the next day. You may look a little dishevelled but you'll be amazed how refreshed you feel, how clear and recalibrated your mind is. The world always seems a better place when you have slept under a canvas of stars, the pleasant ache of miles of trail riding in your legs. There are adventures to be found along every trail, you just need to get into the saddle to find them.